T0193696

a chronological
REVELATION
2ND EDITION

Patterns in Prophecy:

Unveiling God's Design

for the Ages

DAVID KIDD

WESTBOW
PRESS*
A DIVISION OF THOMAS NELSON
& ZONDERVAN

WestBow Press books may be ordered through booksellers or by contacting:

WestBow Press
A Division of Thomas Nelson & Zondervan
1663 Liberty Drive
Bloomington, IN 47403
www.westbowpress.com
1 (866) 928-1240

Cover and interior design by Roy Roper (roy@wideyedesign.net)

ISBN: 978-1-9736-6718-6 (sc)
ISBN: 978-1-9736-6719-3 (hc)
ISBN: 978-1-9736-6717-9 (e)

Library of Congress Control Number: 2019908514

Print information available on the last page.

WestBow Press rev. date: 7/22/2019

CONTENTS

ACKNOWLEDGMENTS

J E S U S , whose sacrifice has given me hope, understanding and life. My wife, Jennifer, whose patience, support and encouragement made this book possible. I have greatly benefited from the editing of my editor, Heidi Walker, and her ability to extract commentary imparting clarity to a very difficult subject. I am thankful as well for all those who read and reflected on the manuscript. Lastly, I am grateful to my good friends Richard Taylor, Don Albright, Greg Crow, Will Hansard and William Mwizerwa for holding me accountable for sharing the understanding God has given me.

PRELUDE TO REVELATION: NATIONAL ISRAEL RETURNS

*Remember this and stand firm, recall it to mind, you
transgressors, remember the former things of old;
for I am God, and there is no other; I am God, and
there is none like me, declaring the end from the beginning
and from ancient times things not yet done, saying,
"My counsel shall stand, and I will accomplish all my purpose."*

ISAIAH 46:8-10

I f you want proof that biblical prophecy can be trusted, you simply have to look at the nation of Israel. By all accounts, this nation should have been wiped off the map years ago. Yet it remains, surrounded by hostile neighbors, and has one of the strongest militaries on earth. Prophets like Jeremiah, Ezekiel, and Isaiah prophesied its rebirth thousands of years ago. Once the Jewish people were scattered in the first century, the rebirth of this nation seemed improbable, even ludicrous. Yet reborn it was.

The rebirth of Israel is also one of the precipitating factors setting the stage for the time of the end. I have always believed that, but my study of Revelation confirmed it. A literal understanding of Israel's rebirth, along with a literal fulfillment of all of the prophecies related to this reborn nation in the end times, support what is an entirely consistent end-times pattern when Revelation is read chronologically.

Consider these verses:

"Who has heard such a thing? Who has seen such things? Shall a land be born in one day? Shall a nation be brought forth in one moment? For as soon as Zion was in labor she brought forth her children" (Isa. 66:8).

"Behold, the days are coming," declares the Lord, "when it shall no longer be said, 'As the Lord lives who brought up the people of Israel out of the land of Egypt,' but 'As the Lord lives who brought up the people of Israel out of the north country and out of all the countries where he had driven them.' For I will bring them back to their own land that I gave to their fathers" (Jer. 16:14-15).

"Behold, I will open your graves and raise you from your graves, O my people. And I will bring you into the land of Israel. And you shall know that I am the Lord, when I open your graves, and raise you from your graves, O my people. And I will put my Spirit within you, and you shall live, and I will place you in your own land. Then you shall know that I am the Lord; I have spoken, and I will do it" (Eze. 37:12-14).

God decreed that there would be a re-establishment of the literal nation of Israel prior to the time of the end. The world witnessed that fulfillment in 1948. The re-establishment of this ancient nation is one of the primary events that sets up the literal fulfillment of all non-symbolic prophecy. Even so, some deny the prophetic importance of the re-established state. To these I must ask, if the reformation of Israel in the twentieth century does not fulfill these prophecies, why did God allow Israel to re-form? God is not a God of confusion (1 Cor. 14:33).

> "'Shall I bring to the point of birth and not cause to bring forth?' says the Lord; 'shall I, who cause to bring forth, shut the womb?' says your God" (Isa. 66:9).

If God decreed that Israel would be brought from the nations of the world to become her own nation again, why do some deny the relevance of the event?

This is not to say that Israel has returned to God spiritually, only that Israel as a nation now exists as foretold. As we shall see in the pages of Revelation and other prophetic books, it is also foretold that, before the final judgment, Israel will return to God spiritually, as well.

As we turn the pages of Revelation, we witness how this transition will take place. As we read how the events unfold, it becomes clear that the return of national Israel is to be taken literally. This is particularly clear as we witness the literal fulfillment of other prophetic passages beginning with the breaking of the second seal.

A CHRONOLOGICAL TEMPLATE

A Chronological Revelation presents a picture of end-times events unlike any other I have come across. By using Revelation as a chronological template and overlaying other prophetic Scriptures, I believe end-times events can be understood in a fresh way. The enigmatic prophecies of Daniel spring to life. The seven-year end of the age becomes part of a larger, intriguing series of events that unravel over a more protracted period of time. We see two major periods of tribulation, one for the church (Matt. 24:9-14) and the other for Israel (Matt. 24:15-28). Throughout these periods, our patient God is actively redeeming his people even as he pours out his increasing wrath on an unrepentant world.

In the pages of this book, I present a view of the end times that I did not anticipate unfolding. I present the book of Revelation beginning with the fifth chapter, passage by passage, and compare it to other prophetic books and discuss how it is consistent with a chronological view. The resulting timeline is illustrated in the chart "A Chronological Revelation." I hope that in sharing this vision of the time of the end, you are encouraged. If you do find yourself living through the events described here, I hope this book will help you find comfort in knowing that God is in complete control and has appointed you for such a time as this.

May you find peace, no matter what circumstances you are facing.

In everything give thanks;
for this is God's will for you in Christ Jesus.

(1 THESS. 5:18 NASB)

INTRODUCTION

But understand this, that in the last days there will come times of difficulty. For people will be lovers of self, lovers of money, proud, arrogant, abusive, disobedient to their parents, ungrateful, unholy, heartless, unappeasable, slanderous, without self-control, brutal, not loving good, treacherous, reckless, swollen with conceit, lovers of pleasure rather than lovers of God, having the appearance of godliness, but denying its power. Avoid such people.

2 TIMOTHY 3:1-5

He said, "Go your way, Daniel, for the words are shut up and sealed until the time of the end. Many shall purify themselves and make themselves white and be refined, but the wicked shall act wickedly. And none of the wicked shall understand, but those who are wise shall understand."

DANIEL 12:9-10

From the time of Jesus' first advent, his followers have sought to understand God's plan for eliminating evil and transitioning them into a perfect relationship with him. Just before his crucifixion, Jesus' disciples asked him about this transition, which Scripture calls "the time of the end." Jesus' response was documented in the Gospels, most prominently in Matthew 24 and 25, but also in Mark 13 and Luke 21. It is interesting to note that John did not address this topic in his gospel account, but later received revelation concerning this time from Jesus. We know this as the book of Revelation.

In the Gospels, the descriptions of the time of the end are relatively short, concise, and straightforward. Revelation is another matter. For centuries scholars, theologians, and the common man have attempted to unravel its mysteries and what has long been accepted to be its symbolic language of seals, beasts, trumpets, witnesses, bowls, and war. According to most accepted interpretations, the events are prophesied in telescoping or recurrent expression. The seven seals, seven trumpets, and seven bowls are alternate descriptions of the same events to one degree or another.

The other book of the Bible that contains the most extensive prophecies concerning the time of the end is Daniel. It, too, features strange beasts, war, and end-times visions. In fact, the visions troubled Daniel so deeply that afterward he said, "So I was left alone and saw this great vision, and no strength was left in me. My radiant appearance was fearfully changed, and I retained no strength" (Dan. 10:8). Other not-yet-fulfilled end-times prophecies are found elsewhere in the Bible. Most notably (although not exclusively), they can be found in the writings of Isaiah, Jeremiah, Ezekiel, and Zechariah.

I originally intended this study to be an informal reading of the book of Revelation in an effort to gain some clarity about a book I had never understood. Early in the process I realized I needed to take notes in order to not get lost...again. But how does one take notes and organize them when one is unsure those notes are being placed in the right order? According to traditional interpretations of Revelation, the notes would be overlapping since the events sometimes appear redundant or outside a normal temporal framework.

Then I began to wonder if, rather than repeating the same events using different imagery, Revelation described these events in the actual order in which they occur. After all, Matthew 24 and 25 seem to describe events in the order in which they unfold, although without the detail and specificity of Revelation. I began by overlaying the events described in Matthew 24 onto Revelation and found that they lined up in perfect chronological order. I took this as confirmation to maintain this process and continued using Revelation as a template. I overlaid other prophecies onto the detailed descriptions in Revelation and found that they, too, were a perfect match.

My study took a very different direction. I was now constrained by what seemed to be one obvious fact: history is told in the sequence in which it unfolds. If prophecy is the pre-telling of history, would it not follow that it would also be told in the sequence in which it will occur? If so, the prophecies in Revelation do not re-tell the same events. They begin with the opening of the first seal in Revelation 5 and end in Revelation 21 with a new heaven and a new earth.

The result is *A Chronological Revelation*, an interpretation that maintains the original sequence of events as described in Revelation and allows other prophetic Scriptures to retain their original sequences as well. What emerges is a beautiful picture of God's repeated calls to repentance prior to his ever-increasing judgment on mankind. I am convinced that God is patiently preparing a great harvest, allowing those who will turn to him to repent in order to spare them from his wrath before the end of the age.

The book of Revelation is not meant to frighten or confuse God's faithful. Rather, it is intended as a warning and call to repentance. It is also intended as a comfort to those who seek to know where they are in the sequence of history. The events described in Revelation are guideposts to reassure those who cry out, "How much longer before you judge and avenge us?" Above all, Revelation establishes that a loving God is, indeed, in control.

MY APPROACH

My training as an architect has taught me to solve problems in a methodical manner, taking into account both functional and aesthetic requirements in order to produce a unified structure. In architecture, the greater the number of parameters that must be considered (including climate, soil conditions, available building materials, build-ing codes, and building type), the greater the challenge of assimi-lating them into a design that accomplishes the goal. Yet it can be done. I applied this same approach to the interpretation of Scripture. If the parameters of God's design for the end of the age are scattered throughout Scripture yet authored by the same omniscient source, it should be possible to compile these texts into one document that re-veals the complete design.

My approach is an honest attempt to let Scripture speak for itself by eliminating all other sources that might pollute its meaning. This approach, I believe, allows us to see what the text is really saying. In my studies, I found that when I could not reconcile a particular point it was generally because I had let the perceptions and interpretations of others creep into my understanding. When I yielded to the text and rejected preconceived or external notions of what the text should say, its meaning became clear. I view this as the Holy Spirit revealing truth.

Was I successful in maintaining this approach 100 percent of the time? Probably not, but the consistency of the patterns that I encountered led me to believe this approach is correct. The more I continue to study Revelation, the more firmly I believe that its events are chronological, even if some of the details need to be refined over time.

This work is an attempt to assimilate all relevant biblical prophecy into one chronological framework. As I use these pages to walk through Revelation, I overlay prophecies from Matthew, Mark, and Luke, as well as from Daniel, Isaiah, Ezekiel, and other prophets, to show how they all work together to create a single, clear, and chronological picture of the time of the end.

To the best of my knowledge, this straightforward overlay approach does not abrogate the orthodox grammatical-historical method of in-terpretation. Nor is there any code or complex symbolism broken here. No esoteric knowledge is required, just a simple, forthright reading of the text under the control of the Holy Spirit. Isn't it just like God to place his revelation right in front of our faces and to open our eyes at his appointed time (Dan. 12:4)?

In short, I believe:

- Jesus foretold history in chronological order, just as is natural when documenting historical events.

- Because all pre-telling of history was authored by the same God, different accounts can be overlaid onto one another without conflict. The result is the revelation of a more complete picture and a confirmation of the sequence.

- Scripture interprets Scripture.

- Language that is clearly symbolic is to be interpreted symbolically. Anything else is to be interpreted literally.

- Symbolic language is consistent throughout the Scriptures.

- Prophecy will be understood ("opened up") at the time of the end.

- These accounts speak solely of the time of the end. They should therefore be interpreted as occurring at a distinct period of time just before Jesus' return.

Some of these discussions may require background not held by every reader. Therefore, to keep the main text simple and easy to read, I interweave important prophecies into the discussion, but for those needing further explanation, I have created short, topic-specific appendixes at the end of the book.

I have also provided a general outline and chart depicting the chronological order of events found in the book of Revelation to assist in maintaining a sense of place as we move through the book.

OUTLINE OF A CHRONOLOGICAL REVELATION

PROLOGUE

Prelude to Revelation: National Israel Returns

A Chronological Template

INTRODUCTION

My Approach

SCROLL AND THE LAMB

Symbolism of the Scroll

Understanding the Beast of Revelation

SEVEN SEALS

First Seal: White Horse (First Head Takes Power)

Second Seal: Red Horse

Third Seal: Black Horse
(First Head Falls / Second, Third, Fourth and Fifth Heads Take Power)
Between Third Seal and Fifth Trumpet

Fourth Seal: Pale Horse

Fifth Seal: Martyred Souls Comforted

Great Tribulation of the True Church /
Great Apostasy of the False Church

Seven Groups of the Elect

Sixth Seal: Those Martyring the Church Fear God's Wrath
(Second, Fourth and Fifth Heads Fall / Sixth Head Takes Power)

INTERLUDE BEFORE THE WRATH

144,000 of Israel Sealed

Multitude out of the Great Tribulation of the Church Given White Robes

Seventh Seal: Silence in Heaven

THE SEVEN TRUMPETS—GOD'S RESTRAINED WRATH

First Trumpet: Earth Struck

Second Trumpet: Sea Struck

Third Trumpet: Water Struck

Fourth Trumpet: Light Struck

Fifth through Seventh Trumpets:
(The Three Woes: Satanic Forces on Earth)

Fifth Trumpet: First Woe

Sixth Trumpet: Second Woe

Israel's Call to Repentance

DANIEL'S SEVENTIETH WEEK BEGINS

Daniel's Fourth Beast (Beast out of the Sea)
(Sixth Head Takes Power Over Ten Horns)

The Lineage of the Antichrist

THE DAY OF THE LORD BEGINS

Seventh Trumpet: The Kingdom of the World
becomes the Kingdom of Our Lord

FIRST THEOLOGICAL INTERLUDE

The Great Signs in Heaven

War in Heaven

Satan Loses Position

The Third Woe

War on Earth: Great Tribulation of Israel

World Government—Beast out of the Sea

World Religion—Beast out of the Earth – False Prophet

World Economic System—
Beast out of the Earth – The Image of The Beast

The Mark of the Beast

REDEMPTION

144,000 Redeemed as Firstfruits

The Harvest of the Earth—Feast of Trumpets

Two Different Experiences of the Harvest

A Closer Look at the Rapture

Martyrdom before Wrath / Rapture before Wrath /
Protection through

Wrath—Always

The 1,335 Days—Yom Kippur

A Picture of God's Faithfulness

Grape Harvest: Winepress of God Commences
(Culminates in Revelation 19:15)

Sea of Glass and Fire—Purification of the Elect

SEVEN BOWLS—GOD'S UNRESTRAINED WRATH

The Bowl Judgments Begin

First Bowl: Painful Sores on Mark Bearers

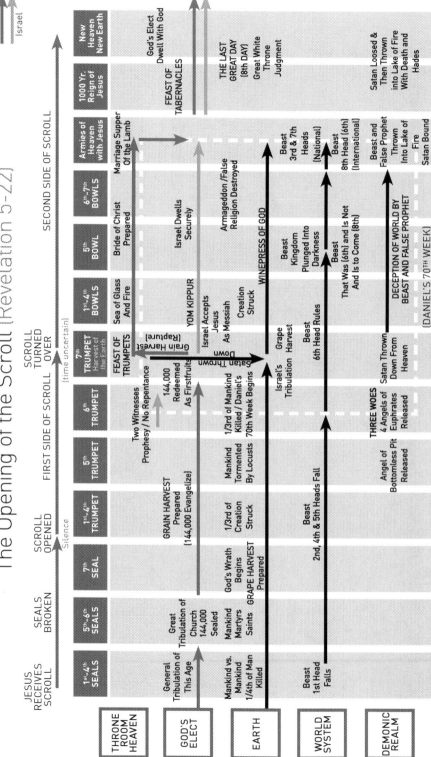

chapter one

THE SCROLL AND THE LAMB

Then I saw in the right hand of him who was seated on the throne
a scroll written within and on the back, sealed with seven seals.
And I saw a strong angel proclaiming with a loud voice, "Who is
worthy to open the scroll and break its seals?" And no one in heaven
or on earth or under the earth was able to open the scroll or to look
into it, and I began to weep loudly because no one was found worthy
to open the scroll or to look into it. And one of the elders said to me,
"Weep no more; behold, the Lion of the tribe of Judah, the Root of David,
has conquered, so that he can open the scroll and its seven seals."

REVELATION 5:1-5

The first four chapters of Revelation have not been included in our discussion since our focus is on the events initiated by the opening of the scroll. It is at this time that "the time of the end" commences and a chronological timeline is established, culminating with the new heaven and new earth. However, because these four chapters provide important background and context for the opening of the scroll as well as characteristics of the church at that time, it is worth providing a short synopsis before continuing our main discussion.

This background and context was revealed to John, who penned Revelation. In Revelation 1, John was told to pass along the contents of the scroll to the seven churches (representing the entirety of the followers of Jesus) in written form. In Revelation 2 and 3, John was told to elaborate on his message to the seven churches by identifying their strengths and weaknesses and their resulting rewards and punishments.

Although these speak to the original churches and various groups within the entire body of Christ, they might also be speaking to the various groups of God's Elect we see at the time of the end. As we will discuss later, while the events of Revelation progress, different groups of God's Elect play unique roles. When overlaying these groups with the characteristics of the seven churches, the chronological pattern matches. The pattern is:

The Church Entering the Time of the End

Ephesus: The Loveless Church (REV. 2:1-7)

The church that has lost its first love and transitioned from faithful to unfaithful is warned to repent prior to entering tribulation at the fifth and sixth seals.

The Martyred Church at the Fifth and Sixth Seals

Smyrna: The Persecuted Church (REV. 2:8-11)

The faithful church emerging out of the loveless church endures tribulation unto death at the fifth and sixth seals.

The Unfaithful Church Descending Deeper Into Apostasy During the Trumpets
(The Woman Riding the Beast, Rev. 17)

Pergamum: The Compromising Church (REV. 2:12-17)

The apostate church surviving the tribulation of the fifth and sixth seals has compromised with the emerging beast system to stay alive. She is called to repent or face Christ's wrath at his second coming.

Thyatira: The Corrupt Church (REV. 2:18-29)

The apostate church has compromised itself into corruption by the beast system. The church is given time to repent but those that do not will enter great tribulation (the bowls).

Sardis: The Dead Church (REV. 3:1-6)

The apostate church so corrupt as to be dead is now totally sold out to the Beast. This church is called to repent and watch or Christ's return will be as a thief, not knowing what hour he comes (missing the rapture / suffering through the bowls).

The Raptured Church at the Seventh Trumpet

Philadelphia: The Faithful Church (REV. 3:7-13)

The church that emerges following the tribulation of the fifth and sixth seals through the ministry of the 144,000 with patient endurance. This church is kept from the hour of trial by being raptured at the seventh trumpet. Those from the apostate churches that repent and remain faithful are also included in this group.

The Church Out of the Bowls Experiencing the First Resurrection

Laodicea: The Lukewarm Church (REV. 3:14-22)

The church uncommitted to either Christ or the Beast misses the rapture at the seventh trumpet and is not kept from the hour of trial (the bowls). This is the final separation of good and evil prior to Christ's return with most taking the Mark of the Beast (being vomited out). Those that do not take the mark of the Beast, thereby answering Jesus' knock on the door, are blessed by being resurrected first and reigning with Christ for one thousand years (Rev. 20:4-5).

These groups of God's Elect are graphically illustrated on the God's Elect chart.

In Revelation 4, John is caught up in the spirit to heaven to the throne of God, where he witnesses the activities to occur just prior to the end of the age. In Revelation 5, the focus turns to the scroll in the right hand of the Father, and we discover that the only one found worthy to open the scroll is Jesus.

> "Worthy are you to take the scroll and to open its seals,
> for you were slain, and by your blood you ransomed people
> for God from every tribe and language and people and nation,
> and you have made them a kingdom and priests to our God,
> and they shall reign on the earth" (Rev. 5:9-10).

This brings us to the beginning of our discussion.

SYMBOLISM OF THE SCROLL

The scroll of Revelation 5 is one of the most recognizable images in all of Revelation. When the Lamb of God is handed the scroll, the stage is set for what follows. It is the precipitating event that enables the final judgment and what many call "the end of the world." Jesus—and only Jesus—is authorized to break the scroll's seals and unleash the series of terrifying events the document foretells.

The opening of the scroll ties together the prophecies of Revelation and those written by the prophet Daniel hundreds of years earlier. In both books, we see Jesus (in Revelation as the Lamb and in Daniel as the Son of Man) being set loose to take his rightful position of kingship over the earth. In both books, we see Jesus destroying his enemies and overpowering and destroying all earthly kingdoms. In both books, we see him setting up his eternal kingdom before judging the living and the dead.

Understanding the parallels between these two books is important because it allows Daniel's prophecies to give us key insights into the enigmatic prophecies of Revelation. This, in turn, gives us a fuller, more detailed picture of the time of the end that helps us appreciate just how sovereign God is over his creation. For those who live to experience these awe-striking prophecies, it also gives them (or perhaps us) the knowledge and confidence needed to understand the events they are about to experience and to stand firm in patience and confidence to endure to the end, no matter how difficult that may seem.

THE STAGE IS SET

With the formation of Israel as a nation in the twentieth century, the stage was set for the end times. Once the seven-sealed scroll is handed to Jesus, the coundown to the end will begin. What irony! The Word of God (John 1:1) brought creation into existence and holds all things in place. Now the very same Word is about to bring an end to all things as we know them, destroying the very creation he once so lovingly spoke into existence.

Jesus has been found worthy to bring this catastrophic judgment because he overcame evil through the sacrifice of his own perfect life. Thus he obtained the right to redeem (harvest) those who share in his victory through faith in him and execute judgment on those who don't.

Let's think for a moment about the imagery found in the sequential breaking of the seals. This imagery is important because it speaks directly to the chronological nature of the events that are about to unfold.

Scrolls were ancient forms of communication for letters and other important documents. Authors often closed their scrolls with wax seals to restrict access to the intended recipient or recipients. In this case, the author is God the Father. The intended recipient is Jesus. Because Jesus is the intended recipient, only he is authorized to break the seals, open the scroll, and unleash the events it describes.

In this case, the breaking of each seal unleashes a new terror upon the world. With the breaking of the first seal, the rise of a formidable national leader ushers in the reign of the beast, the end-time manifestation of evil on a global scale. In the second through fourth seals, this is followed by the rise of global war, global famine, and widespread earthquakes, death, and disease. Perhaps most terrifying, the breaking of the fifth seal allows the inescapable, global persecution of all faithful believers unto death.

Historically, very important documents such as legal contracts, had multiple seals. In this case, the scroll is sealed with seven seals, the biblical number of perfection and completion.

The Scroll of Revelation

As we discuss the imagery of this scroll, it should be noted that there is a fundamental difference between the seals and the contents of the scroll on which they are placed. While the information within the scroll is hidden, the seals, being external, are public in nature. This suggests that the events they unleash, no matter how terrifying, are different from the events written inside the scroll in that they are not unique in history. They have been seen before. The difference is that they occur on a global scale during the end times.

Once the seals are broken, Jesus can open the scroll and unleash its full contents. It might be hard to imagine, but things are about to get much worse. After the seals are broken and the scroll is opened, the seven trumpets are blown. As this occurs, we observe a shift from events previously seen throughout history, even if they are now magnified in scope and intensity, to a new phase of catastrophe far beyond anything man has previously experienced.

The imagery of the scroll is very specific and detailed. This leads one to wonder if the symbolism of the scroll itself is part of the message God is communicating. Some have suggested that the scroll represents the title deed to the earth forfeited at the fall of man in the garden of Eden. I think this interpretation has merit. At the time of the fall, evil entered the world. In Revelation, we see that evil being eliminated. Viewing the scroll as a legal document from both the standoint of its imagery (with its seven seals) and its context (the underlying purpose of restoring mankind to an unblemished relationship with God) lends merit to this interpretation.

In establishing the chronological nature of the events of Revelation, it's crucial to understand how scrolls were historically read. First the exterior seals were broken, one by one. This allowed the scroll to be unrolled and the message inside to be revealed. One side of the scroll would be read (presumably the trumpets), then the scroll would be turned over and the other side would be read (presumably the bowls). This imagery of the seals being broken one by one, followed by the successive reading of each side of the scroll, implies chronology and this supports the view that the events being described in Revelation are chronological.

This is also consistent with the events themselves, which build upon one another as they unfold. The rise of the formidable leader and increasing lawlessness (first seal) leads to raging global war (second seal). It is this global war that leads to global scarcity, disease, and death (seals three and four). The resulting global human crisis opens the door to the rise of the Antichrist and the greatest persecution of believers in history (fifth seal).

As we get further into the book of Revelation, with the blowing of the trumpets and the outpouring of the bowls, we see a similar pattern. The events are sequentially ordered (first trumpet, second trumpet, third trumpet, and so on), with the events unleashed by each judgment building upon one another until they culminate in the battle of Armageddon.

UNDERSTANDING THE BEAST OF REVELATION

Throughout Revelation, evil manifests itself on the earth in the form of a beast. This beast is described in detail in Revelation 13, 17 and Daniel 7. However, since this beast exists in its initial form at the opening of the first seal, it is necessary to briefly discuss its characteristics here.

In Daniel and Revelation, this beast is described as both an individual and a government. This can cause confusion, but the reason is simple. The character of the governmental beast is derived from the character of the individual who leads it. Thus, the term "beast" can refer to both an individual and to the government he leads.

In its governmental form, the beast has seven heads and ten horns. The seven heads represent kings or leaders of the beast in its national form. The horns (nations or regional governments) represent the governmental beast in its international form (an alliance of nations or regions).

The heads rule sequentially, beginning with the rider on the white horse at the first seal and continuing until the return of Christ. Thus their leadership lasts the entire time of the end. The horns—led by the eighth and final beast "head" at Christ's return (Rev. 17:11)—exist as an international alliance, ruling simultaneously beginning sometime after the second seal and extending to the return of Christ. Their control only reaches its zenith just prior to Christ's return.

The beast as an individual is called by various names throughout Scripture. These include the Antichrist, little horn, lawless one, contemptible person, man of lawlessness, son of destruction, king of bold face, and beast from the sea. It is this individual who has spawned countless books, magazine articles, and movies as theologians, authors, and lay believers alike strive to understand and anticipate his terrifying reign.

This individual exists throughout the time of the end, with his power and authority changing throughout the existence of the beast as a governmental form. Beginning at the first seal, it is likely he is working behind the scenes toward the formation of the ten-horned international coalition.

When speaking of the beast throughout this book, the following terms will be used to identify its various manifestations:
- As a nation: "beast nation"
- As an international alliance: "beast alliance"
- As an individual: "little horn" or "Antichrist"
- As all of the above: "beast kingdom" or simply "the beast"

How do we know these things about the beast? By putting together the pieces given to us in Scripture.

The Beast: Mankind's Final World Kingdom

Information on the beast of Revelation can be found in Daniel 2, 7, 8, 11 and Revelation 13, 17. We know these passages speak of the same beast kingdom and that this kingdom exists at the time of the end because it is the final world kingdom that is ultimately destroyed by God (Dan. 2:32-35, Dan. 2:40-45, Dan. 7:26-27, Dan. 8:25, Dan. 11:45, Rev. 13:3-6, Rev. 17:11).

Understanding that these scriptures all speak of the same final, end-times kingdom allow us to identify its specific characteristics. Combining these characteristics reveals its organization.

Beast Nation: Seven Heads

Here is what we know about the beast in its national form:

- This beast has seven heads (Rev. 13:1, Rev. 17:3).

- These seven heads represent sequential leaders of a single nation because we see succession described (Rev. 17:9-11). We also see four kingdoms arising out of what was once one (Dan. 8:21-22).

- This nation originates as the notable horn on the goat of Daniel 8. Here we see a king of bold face who is eventually destroyed by God and arises out of one of the four nations resulting from the break-up of the nation identified as the great or conspicuous horn (Dan. 8:21-25).

- This nation is Western—in other words, from Greek and Roman culture. The goat from which this nation arises comes from the West (Dan. 8:5) and is identified as the king of Greece (Dan. 8:21). In Nebuchadnezzar's image, Greece is associated with bronze, while Rome is associated with iron (Dan. 2:32-35). In Daniel 7, the fourth and final beast is described as having teeth of iron and claws of bronze (Dan. 7:7, 7:19). In Daniel 4 the stump bound with a band of iron and bronze represents the continuation of the Babylonian world political / economic system in its diminished form as Greece and Rome.

- These seven heads rule in succession (Rev. 17:9-11).

- The first head is the first king of Daniel 8. Combining the characteristics found in Daniel 7 and 8 with those of Revelation 17, we can determine that the second, third, fourth, and fifth heads are also four of the ten horns. Knowing that at the appointed time of the end these four heads (horns) come out of the great horn of the goat and three are led by the king of bold face, we can conclude that the first head is the first king of Daniel 8 (Dan. 7:8, Dan. 7:20, Dan. 7:23-24, Dan. 8:8, Dan. 8:20-25, Rev. 17:9-10).

- The second, third, fourth, and fifth heads (horns) arise as the result of the break-up of the notable horn on the goat of Daniel 8 and the loss of power of the first king (Dan. 8:21-22). We can see the demise of these heads in the sequence of leaders of the beast nation described in Revelation 17 (vv. 9-11).

- By taking away the power of the second, fourth, and fifth horns (heads), the sixth head reforms three quarters of the split nation represented by the notable horn on the goat (Dan. 7:8, Dan. 8:22-23). Knowing that the sixth head is the leader who uproots these three horns (heads), it can also be concluded that he is the king of bold face (Dan. 7:8, Dan. 8:22-25, Rev. 17:9-10).

- The third head exists at the time of the fifth bowl (Rev. 17:10).

- The seventh head exists at the time of Christ's return (Rev. 17:10).

- The sixth head returns as an eighth head after losing power at the fifth bowl (Rev. 16:10-11) and leads the ten-horned international alliance at the time of Christ's return (Rev. 17:9-11).

Beast Alliance: Ten Horns

Here is what we know about the beast in its international form:

- This beast has 10 horns (Dan. 7:23-24, Rev. 13:1, Rev. 17:3, Rev.17:12-13) or 10 toes (Dan. 2:40-44).

- These 10 horns (or toes) represent nations or regions led by "kings" (Rev. 17:12-13, Dan. 7:24).

- These 10 horns exist simultaneously (Rev. 17:12-13).

- These 10 horns are controlled by Satan (Rev. 13:1-2).

Since each "king" represents a nation that 1) exists simultaneously with the others, 2) is controlled by Satan, and 3) follows the beast, we know that these horns together represent an international alliance.

Beast Individual: Little Horn or Antichrist

While the beast is described as a nation and an international alliance, the beast is also described as a person (Rev. 13:5, Rev.19:20). It can be inferred by the identification of this individual as the beast that he plays an integral role in the leadership of the governmental forms of the beast.

There is no leader who plays a greater role than the sixth head, whom we have already identified as the little horn (Dan. 7:8) and the king of bold face (Dan. 8:23). With this identification, the actions of this individual provide us with additional details that describe figures elsewhere in Scripture, such as the prince who is to come (Dan. 9:26-27), the contemptible person (Dan. 11:21), the man of lawlessness (2 Thess. 2:4), and the lawless one (2 Thess. 2:8), thus revealing them to be one and the same. This person is most commonly referred to as the Antichrist because he will fully exhibit the characteristics of "the spirit of antichrist" described in 1 and 2 John (1 John 2:18, 1 John 2:22, 1 John 4:3, 2 John 1:7).

For more on identification of the beast, refer to the two theological interlude chapters seven and ten of this book, Appendix A ("Background from Daniel"), and the charts "Prophecy in Daniel," "Revelation's Beast," "The Beast through the Time of the End," and "Daniel Characters in Revelation."

As we conclude the events described in Revelation 5, the Lamb (Jesus) takes the scroll from the Father. The time has finally come for the one who sacrificed everything to receive all for which he sacrificed and truly deserves.

> "Worthy is the Lamb who was slain, to receive power and wealth and wisdom and might and honor and glory and blessing!" (Rev. 5:12).

With this proclamation, worship erupts throughout creation in anticipation of its impending redemption beginning with the opening of the first seal.

chapter two
SEVEN SEALS

Now I watched when the Lamb opened one of the seven seals,
and I heard one of the four living creatures say with a voice
like thunder, "Come!" And I looked, and behold, a white horse!
And its rider had a bow, and a crown was given to him,
and he came out conquering, and to conquer.

REVELATION 6:1-2

The first action most people associate with the book of Revelation is the breaking of the first seal. This initiates a series of events that culminates with the end of this age. Like many of the events detailed in Revelation, however, "the end of the age" is multi-phased.

The terms used by the prophets for events that build up to the end of the age, culminating in the second coming of Christ, include "the time of the end" and "the end." The time of the end is a broad period that extends from the breaking of the first seal to the seventh trumpet and includes many warnings of the coming judgment. At the seventh trumpet, we move from the time of the end to the end itself, a period that begins with Satan being thrown out of heaven and extends through the bowls to the second coming of Christ.

Understanding the time of the end is critical because Jesus said it will be characterized by deception. This is a time when believers will need to know—*really* know—the true from the false because there will be many who will come in his name and try to lead them astray.

> "For many will come in my name, saying 'I am the Christ,' and they will lead many astray" (Matt. 24:5; cf. Mark 13:6; Luke 21:8).

How will we know the true from the false? By knowing the Scriptures. Although there are some truths that God has chosen to veil in mystery, those things we can know go all the way back to the writings of the prophet Daniel and are recorded by Isaiah, Zechariah and other minor prophets.

So that we may know the truth, we will look first at the seals of Revelation, then overlay them onto the earlier prophecies so that we may gain a fuller picture of what these times will be like.

First Seal
WHITE HORSE
(First Head Takes Power)

At the breaking of the first seal we are introduced to a rider, a powerful character who plays a critical role in the unfolding of all the events about to follow. He is a form of antichrist (although not the Antichrist) and is the same character we meet in one of the terrifying visions given to the prophet Daniel (Dan 8:21) back in the sixth century B.C. Described as the "first king", this rider, who is given a crown, is a political leader who brings the promise of peace and revived prosperity to a world on the brink of political and economic collapse. While many people see this rider as the Antichrist, he is more likely a figure who lays the foundation for the Antichrist who is to come.

At the time the first seal is broken, the world will be descending into chaos. Although not overtly stated, this is strongly suggested by the symbolism of the white horse, the proclamation of peace, and the details provided in Daniel 8 (see discussion at the second seal). In the midst of this turmoil, this rider will proclaim a new world order that will resolve the inequities and failings of the existing one. This is a counterfeit of Jesus and his promised millennial reign foretold in Revelation 20. By acting in this role, this leader offers himself as a messianic substitute. While the rider of the first seal may not make this claim overtly, it is a claim nonetheless. This is evident by the symbolism of the white horse, which is how Jesus is depicted at his second coming to set up his kingdom.

This rider of the first seal is seen elsewhere in Revelation. As previously noted, the beast kingdom has a national component represented by seven heads. These seven heads are seven leaders of a single nation who rule sequentially. The fact that they are sequential in nature is drawn from Revelation 17's description of the scarlet beast. This description includes ten horns on the heads. These ten horns tie the vision of the scarlet beast back to another end-times beast—the one found in Daniel 7:

> "After this I saw in the night visions, and behold, a fourth beast, terrifying and dreadful and exceedingly strong. It had great iron teeth; it devoured and broke in pieces and stamped what was left with its feet. It was different from all the beasts that were before it, and it had ten horns" (Dan. 7:7).

This fourth beast, with its ten horns, is one and the same as the scarlet beast in Revelation 17. This description gives us more insight into what the character of the seven end-times leaders of this wicked beast nation will be like. These will be brutal dictators bent on destroying the people of God.

As we overlay the Scriptures, we see that the rider of the white horse in the first seal is also the first of seven leaders who will rule this beast nation during the end times. This nation does not necessarily come into existence during the end times It simply takes on the character and role of the beast at the time of the end. The first seal is the beginning of this nation's role as the beast as represented by the coming of the first head on a white horse. Ultimately, this leader's failure (possibly intentional) to maintain the existing world order leads to war, economic collapse, and a new world order dominated by the beast nation.

Despite the appearance of imminent total world collapse, the new world order initiated by the first leader of the beast kingdom, and perpetuated by the dominance of the nation he leads, is just getting started. As we will see, the result of this deception is partially realized at the breaking of the fifth and sixth seals when the intense, global persecution led by another key figure of Revelation, the false prophet, causes an apostasy of the unfaithful church.

To help us see the chronology unfolding here, let's overlay the first seal with the parallel verses in the Gospels:

Revelation

"I watched as the Lamb opened the first of the seven seals. Then I heard one of the four living creatures say in a voice like thunder, "Come!" I looked, and there before me was a white horse! Its rider held a bow, and he was given a crown, and he rode out as a conqueror bent on conquest" (Rev. 6:1-2).

Gospels

"For many will come in my name, saying 'I am the Christ,' and they will lead many astray" (Matt. 24:5).

"Many will come in my name, claiming, 'I am he,' and will deceive many" (Mark 13:6).

"He replied: 'Watch out that you are not deceived. For many will come in my name, claiming, "I am he," and, "The time is near." Do not follow them'" (Luke 21:8).

Second Seal
RED HORSE

At the breaking of the second seal, the current world order has collapsed (see discussion on Daniel 8 below) and the world is descending into war. We can see details of this collapse and the rise of global unrest by comparing the prophecy of the second seal with the parallel accounts in the Gospels. Just as the first seal parallels Matthew 24:5, Mark 13:6, and Luke 21:8, the second seal parallels the events in the verses immediately following:

Revelation

"When he opened the second seal, I heard the second living creature say, 'Come!' And out came another horse, bright red. Its rider was permitted to take peace from the earth" (Rev. 6:3-4).

Gospels

"And you will hear of wars and rumors of war. See that you are not alarmed, for this must take place, but the end is not yet. For nation will rise against nation, and kingdom against kingdom" (Matt. 24:6-7).

"And when you hear of wars and rumors of wars, do not be alarmed. This must take place, but the end is not yet. For nation will rise against nation, and kingdom against kingdom" (Mark 13:7-8).

"And when you hear of wars and tumults, do not be terrified, for these things must first take place, but the end will not be at once." Then he said to them, 'Nation will rise against nation, and kingdom against kingdom'" (Luke 21:9-10).

We are given additional details of the period of the second seal in the book of Daniel. The collapse of the existing world order is initiated by the events foretold in Daniel 8 and now being fulfilled. Let's look at Daniel's description of this time:

"I raised my eyes and saw, and behold, a ram standing on the bank of the canal. It had two horns, and both horns were high, but one was higher than the other, and the higher one came up last. I saw the ram charging westward and northward and southward. No beast could stand before him, and there was no one who could rescue from his power. He did as he pleased and became great. As I was considering, behold, a male goat came from the west across the face of the whole earth, without touching the ground. And the goat had a conspicuous horn between his eyes. He came to the ram with the two horns, which I had seen standing on the bank of the canal, and he ran at him in his powerful wrath. I saw him come close to the ram, and he was enraged against him and struck the ram and broke his two horns. And the ram had no power to stand before him, but he cast him down to the ground and trampled on him. And there was no one who could rescue the ram from his power" (Dan. 8:3-7).

The "conspicuous horn" (Dan. 8:5) is called "the notable horn" in other translations. We will be referring to this horn throughout this book because just as heads represent national leaders in biblical prophecy, horns tend to represent nations or significant leaders wielding power. As we will see, the notable horn refers to the beast nation in its original form.

This prophecy has a partial fulfillment in the ancient kingdoms of Greece and Medo-Persia. However, based on Daniel 8:17 and Daniel 8:19, this vision is tied to the time of the end. Therefore we know that this prophecy must have a future (and perfect) fulfillment as well as an historical one. I have outlined both the past and future fulfillments of this prophecy below:

Vision	First Fulfillment	Future Fulfillment
Goat	The Kingdom of Greece	Western Civilization (a coalition)
Ram	Medes and Persians	Possibly the Kurds and Iran or the Ram could be modern Iran with the ancient Medes assimilated into its population.
Notable Horn	First King / Alexander the Great	Possibly the United States without the Constitution and with the rider on the white horse as the first king

From a future perspective, the Kurds (modern-day Medes?) and Iran (modern-day Persia or simply Iran with its assimilated ancient Mede population) constitute the ram. From this prophecy, we know that the ram moves out of Iran westward into Iraq and possibly Jordan, then northward into northern Iraq, eastern Turkey, and perhaps the Caucasus. Then it moves southward toward Kuwait and Saudi Arabia (Dan. 8:4). The westward move threatens Israel, while the southward move threatens the goat (Greece) economically due to the vast oil resources in Kuwait and Saudi Arabia.

Because Daniel 8:17 and Daniel 8:19 place this prophecy at the time of the end, we must seek to understand the modern-day identification of the kingdom of Greece. I believe the term "kingdom of Greece" is used purposefully to distinguish the *nation* of Greece from the *culture* of Greece. Even the symbolism of the animals (the ram and goat, representing their constituent nations' character or culture) and the horns (representing individual nations) support this approach.

In the modern world, it is quite evident that the Greek culture has survived throughout Europe and North America. Today we call this region "the West." We must then search out the most dominant nation within this culture to identify the notable horn. At this time, I believe we would be very much justified in looking at the United States. I am not dogmatic on this point, but for purposes of this book, I will use the United States as the fulfillment of this prophecy even though ultimately another nation may take this role. Other horns represent major countries in Europe and North America, but one will be dominating and leading them. Again, while for purposes of discussion it will be assumed that the United States fulfills this role, this identification is not dogmatic since this prophecy could refer to a more distant future fulfillment.

As the notable horn, the United States (Dan. 8:5) and its Western coalition partners (the goat) will respond to Iran's (the ram's) attack by long-range bomber or missile attack from bases within the United States, literally "crossing the whole earth without touching the ground" (Dan. 8:5). Whether the U.S.-led coalition uses long-range missiles because the nations are hampered economically or militarily (perhaps as the result of a terrorist attack, natural disaster or internal conflict) or whether they simply are required to strike without warning, such as to prevent a nuclear launch by Iran on Israel, we are not told.

> "And the goat is the king of Greece. And the great horn between
> his eyes is the first king" (Dan. 8:21).

When Daniel says "the first king," he is referring to ," he ," the first head of the beast nation, or the rider of the first seal. Because the kingdom of Greece is now what we refer to as "the West," we are being told that the rider of the first seal is from the West. The fact that Daniel calls him a "king" rather than a "head" suggests that something occurs to allow this Western leader to move from democratic to dictatorial power. Assuming this is the United States, this means that, at some point, the United States will lose its republic, much as ancient Rome lost its republic. Likewise, just as Rome's loss of its republic allowed the rise of the autocratic position of emperor, the United States' loss of its republic opens the door to autocratic leadership and its role as the beast nation.

Many scholars believe the goat in this passage has a historic fulfillment in the conquests of Alexander the Great, who conquered Persia (modern-day Iran) in the fourth century B.C. If this passage did, in fact, reference a historical fulfillment only, this would create a problem because Alexander the Great was not the first king of Greece. He was actually the second king following Phillip, his father. If you hold to a modern-day fulfillment by the United States, one only has to wait for a perfect fulfillment since the United States has not yet had a king. In order for this prophecy to be fulfilled, the Constitution must be abrogated as the United States loses its republican form of government and allows someone to gain dictatorial power.

With the "first king," identified as the rider on the white horse (a leader who enters the world scene proclaiming peace), the war at the second seal marks his domination by force. This is suggested by his possession of a bow. This is made possible because this rider has received royal authority ("a crown was given to him").

As scary as these events may seem, the end is not yet. Nor will it all come at once (Luke 21:9). This is another hint that we can expect a protracted set of events before Christ's return.

Third Seal
BLACK HORSE
**(First Head Falls / Second, Third, Fourth, and Fifth Heads
Take Power Between Third Seal and Fifth Trumpet)**

"When he opened the third seal, I heard the third living creature say, 'Come!' And I looked, and behold, a black horse! And its rider had a pair of scales in his hand. And I heard what seemed to be a voice in the midst of the four living creatures, saying, 'A quart of wheat for a denarius, and three quarts of barley for a denarius, and do not harm the oil and wine!'" (Rev. 6:5-6).

"Then the goat became exceedingly great, but when he was strong, the great horn was broken, and instead of it there came up four conspicuous horns toward the four winds of heaven…. As for the horn that was broken, in place of which four others arose, four kingdoms shall arise from his nation, but not with his power" (Dan. 8:8, 22).

At the breaking of the third seal, the world will be recovering from war and in the midst of political and economic collapse. Simultaneous disruption of the world's supply chain and collapse of fiat currencies due to debasement results in an inflationary depression, or hyper stagflation. A severe shortage of goods accompanies the destruction of savings and employment income leading to unimaginable poverty worldwide.

At this time, the United States will break into four separate regional governments as a result of internal strife (Dan. 8:8). Ultimately, although not actually seen in Revelation until the sixth trumpet, the Antichrist will emerge from one of the resulting four regions and reunite three of them into a post-Constitution, Re-United States without the constraints of the Constitution (Dan. 8:9). This Antichrist will be destroyed at Christ's return. The identity of the Antichrist will be addressed in the discussion of the seventh trumpet in Revelation 13.

Somewhere between the breaking of the third seal and the blowing of the fifth trumpet, the first head of the beast nation loses power. He is replaced by the second, third, fourth, and fifth heads, which exist simultaneously as the heads of the four separate regional governments of the nation Daniel saw in his vision as the notable horn on the goat.

To fully understand the sequence of these events, we must combine the information given to us in Revelation 17:9-10 and Daniel 8:8, 22. When overlaying these prophecies, the pattern of the seven heads of the beast nation becomes clear. I place the loss of power of the rider of the first seal here, at the time of the third seal, because it is likely that the demise of the nation he leads coincides with the stresses brought on by the breakdown of the existing world order. To date I have found no prophecy to precisely locate this event. The only firm time marker we are given is when the fifth head eventually loses power prior to the time described in Revelation 17 (see commentary on Revelation 17:9-10).

Fourth Seal
PALE HORSE

> "When he opened the fourth seal, I heard the voice of the fourth living creature say, "Come!" And I looked, and behold, a pale horse! And its rider's name was Death, and Hades followed him. And they were given authority over a fourth of the earth, to kill with sword and with famine and with pestilence and by wild beasts of the earth" (Rev. 6:7-8).

As a result of the severe global scarcity of goods during the third seal, Scripture tells us that one-quarter of mankind will be killed by one of four deadly forces:

- **Man:** In an attempt to stay alive, mankind will take from and kill others.
- **Famine:** Severe food shortages will cause many deaths.
- **Disease:** The compromised natural environment will invite disease.
- **Wild animals:** The struggle for food will set up competition between man and animals.

Jesus makes these same prophecies in the Gospels. Once again, we have a parallel between Revelation and the Gospels that supports the consecutive nature of these events:

Revelation

> "When he opened the fourth seal, I heard the voice of the fourth living creature say, 'Come!' And I looked, and behold, a pale

horse! And its rider's name was Death, and Hades followed him. And they were given authority over a fourth of the earth, to kill with sword and with famine and with pestilence and by wild beasts of the earth" (Rev. 6:7-8).

Gospels

"And there will be famines and earthquakes in various places. All these are but the beginnings of birth pains" (Matt. 24:7-8).

"There will be earthquakes in various places; there will be famines. These are but the beginning of the birth pains" (Mark 13:8).

"There will be great earthquakes, and in various places famines and pestilences" (Luke 21:11).

At this point, collapse of the existing world order is complete. Although there are a number of prophecies yet to be fulfilled before the complete dominance of the beast nation, the stage is now set. Before this happens, we see the rise of one of the most fearsome individuals in end-times prophecy, the false prophet. He unleashes the greatest persecution of Christians the world has ever seen.

Fifth Seal
MARTYRED SOULS COMFORTED

"When he opened the fifth seal, I saw under the altar the souls of those who had been slain for the word of God and for the witness they had borne. They cried out with a loud voice, "O Sovereign Lord, holy and true, how long before you will judge and avenge our blood on those who dwell on the earth?" Then they were each given a white robe and told to rest a little longer, until the number of their fellow servants and their brothers should be complete, who were to be killed as they themselves had been" (Rev. 6:9-11).

With the opening of the fifth seal, we see the martyrs throughout history crying out to God for vengeance. As they do, we see a critical transition occurring. We see the transition from the martyrdom that has occurred during the *general tribulation* of this age to the intense, global, and inescapable martyrdom that comprises the *great tribulation of the church* that is blamed for the horrific events of the first four seals. The purpose of the opening of the heavenly realm is to provide comfort to readers who may live to see these times and be the very ones to undergo this intense persecution.

The desire of the martyred saints for God's judgment is met with his assurance that such judgment is coming. God then provides for the soon-to-be glorified bodies of these saints by giving each of them a white robe. These robes signify the start of another phase of God's plan, a phase in which all faithful believers undergo persecution unto death. In his mercy, God will allow people to come to saving faith during this time, but martyrdom will ultimately follow.

GREAT TRIBULATION OF THE TRUE CHURCH
GREAT APOSTASY OF THE FALSE CHURCH

"He who now restrains it [lawlessness] will do so until He is taken away" (2 Thess. 2:7).

"Let no one deceive you in any way. For that day will not come, unless the rebellion [falling away] comes first and the man of lawlessness is revealed" (2 Thess. 2:3).

Until this point, there were two churches present upon the earth: the faithful church (the body of Christ) and the apostate church. But now, the last member of the faithful church will have been killed. This will leave the apostate church as the only "church" on the earth. Who will these people be? There is a large contingent attending churches today who will fall away because they don't believe Jesus is the only way to God. As the earth suffers under the devastating plagues of the seals, and as the persecution comes, those people will be revealed. They may still continue to attend church, but this will not be the true church of God. The deception during this time will be so great that those killing the saints will believe that they are offering service to God (John 16:2).

This mass "falling away" from the true faith, or apostasy, is the first of two signs given in 2 Thessalonians 2:1-4 that must occur prior to the day of the Lord. This day will be discussed in detail at its beginning in Revelation 11. The second sign, the revealing of the man of lawlessness, will occur when Israel flees into the wilderness at the abomination of desolation (Rev. 12:16).

Although many will expect to see the return of Christ immediately following the events of the first four seals, Scripture tells us that this will not happen. This delay will fuel mankind in turning on those who warned of imminent judgment. The world will be deceived into believing they are doing God's will by eliminating the followers of Jesus who, they believe, hold to this divisive "delusion" of his physical return. In this, they will repeat the pattern of the Jews and the church in the first century (John 16:1-4).

> "I have said all these things to you to keep you from falling away. They will put you out of the synagogues. Indeed, the hour is coming when whoever kills you will think he is offering service to God. And they will do these things because they have not known the Father, nor me. But I have said these things to you, that when their hour comes you may remember that I told them to you" (John 16:1-4).

Under intense persecution and threat of death, the true, faithful church will endure unto death. Those who falsely claim the faith will fall away, forsaking Jesus and becoming part of the apostate church. The false prophet and the woman described in Revelation 17 will lead this apostasy. A common cry of the persecutors will be in essence, "Where is your Savior? We're killing you and he fails to return to stop us." This will lead to further fulfillment of 2 Peter 3:3-4:

> "Knowing this first of all, that scoffers will come in the last days with scoffing, following their own sinful desires. They will say, 'Where is the promise of his coming? For ever since the fathers fell asleep, all things are continuing as they were from the be-

ginning of creation.'"

This is one of the dangers of pretribulation rapture eschatology. This view holds that Jesus will not allow his church to undergo global persecution. As a result, many Christians will be counting on protection from this martyrdom. When that protection does not come, many will fall away without ever experiencing the transforming power that comes from true faith: "But you will receive power when the Holy Spirit has come upon you, and you will be my witnesses in Jerusalem and in all Judea and Samaria, and to the end of the earth" (Acts 1:8). Anticipation of this tribulation can be further found in Revelation 1:9, where John proclaims himself as our brother in tribulation. Despite the continuing operation of the apostate church, the willingness of the true church to be faithful unto death will be a profound witness to the entire world.

Jesus spoke of this tribulation and martyrdom in the Gospels, as well.

Gospels

"Then they will deliver you up to tribulation and put you to death, and you will be hated by all nations *for my name's sake*. And then many will fall away and betray one another and hate one another. And many false prophets will arise and lead many astray. And because lawlessness will be increased, the love of many will grow cold. But the one who endures to the end will be saved. And this gospel of the kingdom will be proclaimed throughout the whole world as a testimony to all nations, and then the end will come" (Matt. 24:9-14, emphasis mine).

"But be on your guard. For they will deliver you over to councils, and you will be beaten in synagogues, and you will stand before governors and kings for my sake, to bear witness before them. And the gospel must first be proclaimed to all nations....And you will be hated by all *for my name's sake*. But the one who endures to the end will be saved" (Mark 13:9-13, emphasis mine).

"But before all this they will lay their hands on you and persecute you, delivering you up to the synagogues and prisons, and you will be brought before kings and governors *for my name's sake*. This will be your opportunity to bear witness....You will be delivered up even by parents and brothers and relatives and friends, and some of you they will put to death. You will be hated by all *for my name's sake*. But not a hair of your head will perish. By your endurance you will gain your lives" (Luke 21:12-19, emphasis mine).

What a promise for those to be martyred! While Jesus seems to offer the promise of physical protection by stating "not a hair on your head" will perish, in the larger context, he is clearly talking about protection into eternal life, not protection of the physical body. Even so, this is an incredible, comforting promise that is repeated in Revelation 2:10: "Be faithful even to the point of death, and I will give you the crown of life."

Anyone can receive the gospel with gladness. It is only the truly faithful—those rooted in the foundation of Christ—who endure during the most difficult times. Only those who truly know God can withstand the pressure of persecution. It is this endurance that God uses to test our faith.

> "As for what was sown on rocky ground, this is the one who hears the word and immediately receives it with joy, yet he has no root in himself, but endures for a while, and when tribulation or persecution arises on account of the word, immediately he falls away" (Matt. 13:20-21).

In stark contrast, those who know Christ and are rooted in him have a peace and steadfastness that will overcome this persecution and bring glory to his name.

> "I have said these things to you, that in me you may have peace. In the world you will have tribulation. But take heart; I have overcome the world" (John 16:33).

> "Who shall separate us from the love of Christ? Shall tribulation, or distress, or persecution, or famine, or nakedness, or danger,

or sword?" (Rom. 8:35).

"Rejoice in hope, be patient in tribulation, be constant in prayer" (Rom. 12:12).

"I tell you, my friends, do not fear those who kill the body, and after that have nothing more that they can do. But I will warn you whom to fear: fear him who, after he has killed, has authority to cast into hell. Yes, I tell you, fear him!" (Luke 12:4-5).

"And I tell you, everyone who acknowledges me before men, the Son of Man also will acknowledge before the angels of God, but the one who denies me before men will be denied before the angels of God. And everyone who speaks a word against the Son of Man will be forgiven, but the one who blasphemes against the Holy Spirit will not be forgiven. And when they bring you before the synagogues and the rulers and the authorities, do not be anxious about how you should defend yourself or what you should say, for the Holy Spirit will teach you in that very hour what you ought to say" (Luke 12:8-12).

Although all true followers of Jesus will have been martyred by this time, God will not be left without a witness. At this point, he seals the 144,000, protecting them from death, and they will survive as continuing witnesses through the trumpet judgments. This yields another great harvest that is gathered at the seventh trumpet upon Jesus' return. This event is commonly referred to as the rapture.

It must be mentioned that the great tribulation of the church we have been discussing is different from the great tribulation of Israel (Daniel's Seventieth Week), which is referred to beginning in Matthew 24:15. The great tribulation of Israel will occur at the blowing of the sixth trumpet and will be discussed in further detail later in this book.

SEVEN GROUPS OF THE ELECT

This distinction between the great tribulation of the *church* and the great tribulation of *Israel* is the first reference to distinct groups of God's elect defined by events in Revelation. I believe one of the keys to understanding Revelation is realizing that God is dealing with different groups of his elect in different ways, not simply removing his entire church at a single moment at the rapture. These groups are created as the events of Revelation unfold and they play very specific roles as God's witness throughout the time of the end.

Listed below is a preview of these groups. Their timeline can be found on the chart "God's Elect," as well.

- Martyrs out of the general tribulation of this age (fifth through sixth seals)

- Martyrs out of the great tribulation of the church (fifth through sixth seals)

- 144,000 of Israel (sixth seal / seventh trumpet)

- Believers throughout this age and those out of the first five trumpet judgments (seventh trumpet / rapture)

- Remnant of Israel (seventh trumpet)

- Believers not taking the mark of the beast (first through third bowls / first resurrection through Rev. 20:4-6)

- Believers out of the millennial reign of Christ (second resurrection)

Sixth Seal
THOSE MARTYRING THE CHURCH FEAR GOD'S WRATH

"When he opened the sixth seal, I looked, and behold, there was a great earthquake, and the sun became black as sackcloth, the full moon became like blood, and the stars of the sky fell to the earth as the fig tree sheds its winter fruit when shaken by a gale. The sky vanished like a scroll that is being rolled up, and every mountain and island was removed from its place. Then the kings of the earth and the great ones and the generals and the rich and the powerful, and everyone, slave and free, hid themselves in the caves and among the rocks of the mountains, calling to the mountains and rocks, 'Fall on us and hide us from the face of him who is seated on the throne, and from the wrath of the Lamb, for the great day of their wrath has come, and who can stand?'" (Rev. 6:12-17).

"And there will be terrors and great signs from heaven" (Luke 21:11).

"The sun shall be turned to darkness, and the moon to blood, before the great and awesome day of the Lord comes" (Joel 2:31).

"The sun shall be turned to darkness and the moon to blood, before the day of the Lord comes, the great and magnificent day" (Acts 2:20).

As we can see from the cry, "Hide us from the face of him who is seated on the throne!" those who have just lived through the first five seals view these events as a sign. This sign, they believe, signals that God is judging the world for killing his followers and that this is the end. When this expectation is not immediately met and the end does not come, they are confirmed in their disbelief and their response is to return to their rebellious lives.

However, these signs do portend judgement, particularly the sun turning to sackcloth and moon to blood, because they herald the Day of the Lord (Joel 2:31, Acts 2:20), a most auspicious time of God's punishment.

Yet believers will find trust and hope in the Lord, for he has told them in advance what will happen. Though they may lose their lives, he has promised that their futures are secure.

"God is our refuge and strength, a very present help in trouble. Therefore we will not fear though the earth gives way, though the mountains be moved into the heart of the sea, though its waters roar and foam, though the mountains tremble at its swelling. *Selah*" (Psalm 46:1-3).

chapter three

INTERLUDE BEFORE THE WRATH

144,000 OF ISRAEL SEALED

After this I saw four angels standing at the four corners of the earth, holding back the four winds of the earth, that no wind might blow on earth or sea or against any tree. Then I saw another angel ascending from the rising of the sun, with the seal of the living God, and he called with a loud voice to the four angels who had been given power to harm earth and sea, saying, 'Do not harm the earth or the sea or the trees, until we have sealed the servants of our God on their foreheads.' And I heard the number of the sealed, 144,000, sealed from every tribe of the sons of Israel: 12,000 from the tribe of Judah were sealed, 12,000 from the tribe of Reuben, 12,000 from the tribe of Gad, 12,000 from the tribe of Asher, 12,000 from the tribe of Naphtali, 12,000 from the tribe of Manasseh, 12,000 from the tribe of Simeon, 12,000 from the tribe of Levi, 12,000 from the tribe of Issachar, 12,000 from the tribe of Zebulun, 12,000 from the tribe of Joseph, 12,000 from the tribe of Benjamin were sealed.

REVELATION 7:1-8

Be patient, therefore, brothers, until the coming of the Lord. See how the farmer waits for the precious fruit of the earth, being patient about it, until it receives the early and late rains.

JAMES 5:7

J ames tells us that between his time and the coming of the Lord there will be two rains, an early rain and a late rain. "Rain" here symbolizes the work of the Holy Spirit in preparation for the harvest of believers to come. Revelation 7 marks the end of the early rain, which began at Pentecost, and the beginning of the late rain, which begins with the filling of 144,000 Jewish witnesses with the Holy Spirit (an event foreshadowed by Pentecost). This rain produces a great harvest at the seventh trumpet.

As we will see later, the 144,000 are protected during the blowing of the seven trumpets. Although we aren't specifically told why they are protected, it is likely to bear witness to the world. In this, they parallel their counterparts at Pentecost who, as the early rain, were the firstfruits of the gospel. As the late rain, the 144,000 bear witness during the time of the end, and because of their faithfulness, they will ultimately be offered up as firstfruits on Mount Zion (Rev. 14:1-5). Together, the martyred church and the 144,000 witnesses represent the entirety of the elect at this time.

MULTITUDE OUT OF GREAT TRIBULATION GIVEN WHITE ROBES

In Revelation 7:9-14, we see that while these believers give up their lives during the great tribulation, they are given great glory and honor in heaven.

> "After this I looked, and behold, a great multitude that no one could number, from every nation, from all tribes and peoples and languages, standing before the throne and before the Lamb, clothed in white robes, with palm branches in their hands, and crying out with a loud voice, 'Salvation belongs to our God who sits on the throne, and to the Lamb!' And all the angels were standing around the throne and around the elders and the four living creatures, and they fell on their faces before the throne and worshiped God, saying, 'Amen! Blessing and glory and wisdom and thanksgiving and honor and power and might be to our God forever and ever! Amen.'"

"Then one of the elders addressed me, saying, 'Who are these, clothed in white robes, and from where have they come?' I said to him, 'Sir, you know.' And he said to me, 'These are the ones coming out of the great tribulation. They have washed their robes and made them white in the blood of the Lamb.'"

That all believers alive at this time (excluding the 144,000) will be martyred is decidedly uncomfortable for most people, but Scripture is clear on this point. While this may seem frightening, it is important to understand that it is part of the sovereign plan of God. Therefore, if we are counted among them, we can have the kind of peace that helps us to endure.

This knowledge should be a great encouragement to all who find themselves appointed to live during the end times. Look at what the angel has to say about the future of this group of elect:

"They shall hunger no more, neither thirst anymore; the sun shall not strike them, nor any scorching heat. For the Lamb in the midst of the throne will be their shepherd, and he will guide them to springs of living water, and God will wipe away every tear from their eyes" (Rev. 7:16-17).

SEVENTH SEAL: SILENCE IN HEAVEN

We now reach the breaking of the seventh and final seal. With it comes one of the most ominous events described in Revelation: utter silence in heaven as God prepares to pour out his wrath upon an unrepentant world.

"When the Lamb opened the seventh seal, there was silence in heaven for about half an hour. Then I saw the seven angels who stand before God, and seven trumpets were given to them. And another angel came and stood at the altar with a golden censer, and he was given much incense to offer with the prayers of all the saints on the golden altar before the throne, and the smoke of the incense, with the prayers of the saints, rose before God from the hand of the angel. Then the angel took the censer and filled it with fire from the altar and threw it on the earth, and there were peals of thunder, rumblings, flashes of lightning, and an earthquake" (Rev. 8:1-5).

The last seal has been broken and the contents of the interior of the scroll are about to be revealed. The martyrdom of the saints has kindled God's wrath, and all of heaven is in silent awe of what is about to take place. God has saved up all the prayers for justice that have been uttered throughout history. He now prepares for his execution of this judgment by providing his angels with trumpets to signal the onset of each event. God's plan for his elect is graphically depicted in the attached chart, "God's Elect."

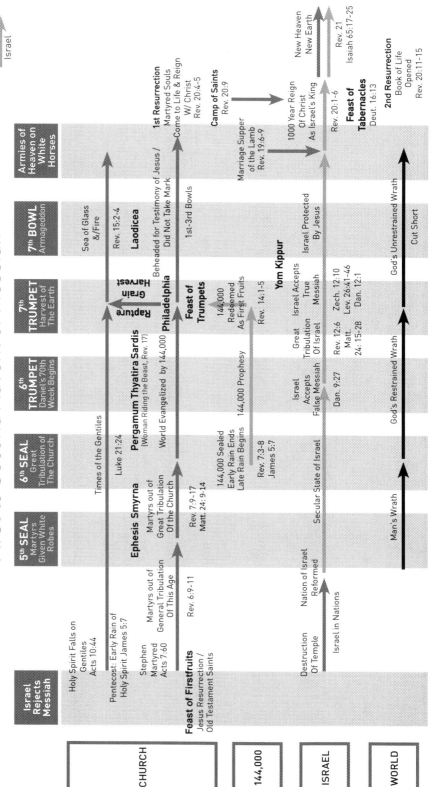

GOD'S ELECT
First to Second Advent of Messiah

chapter four

SEVEN TRUMPETS GOD'S RESTRAINED WRATH

Now the seven angels who had
the seven trumpets prepared to blow them.

REVELATION 8:6

At this point in Revelation, we are about to understand why heaven was silent for half an hour. The blowing of the trumpets commences. Those who thought that things could not possibly get worse than the terrifying and cataclysmic events unleashed by the seals are about to find out that they can—and they do. As the trumpets are blown, we begin to witness the horrifying events of God's wrath.

One thing that is important to notice, however, is that while this period of systematic destruction will be horrific, God still shows restraint by limiting the destruction to one-third of the affected portions of creation. We will not speculate on how these attacks will be accomplished, only to say that, like the other events of Revelation, it is likely they will be fulfilled literally.

Although the "early rain" believers have been martyred, people will still be saved during this time. Through the first five trumpets, God continues to redeem new faithful through the witness of the 144,000. These followers will experience unjust persecution at the hands of mankind just as their predecessors did in the first century, but they will be rewarded for their faithfulness by avoiding the events of the bowl judgments (God's unrestrained wrath) and with everlasting life.

First Trumpet
EARTH STRUCK

"The first angel blew his trumpet, and there followed hail and fire, mixed with blood, and these were thrown upon the earth. And a third of the earth was burned up, and a third of the trees were burned up, and all green grass was burned up" (Rev. 8:7).

The first trumpet releases hail, fire, and blood that destroys one-third of the vegetation. This begins the systematic degradation of the earth's ecosystem by reducing its capacity to produce food and oxygen and by disrupting its wildlife habitat. Ultimately, these events have tragic consequences.

Second Trumpet
SEA STRUCK

"The second angel blew his trumpet, and something like a great mountain, burning with fire, was thrown into the sea, and a third of the sea became blood. A third of the living creatures in the sea died, and a third of the ships were destroyed" (Rev. 8:8-9).

The second trumpet releases an event described by the apostle John as being "like a burning mountain" falling into the sea. This results in the destruction of one-third of the sea creatures and ships. As in the first trumpet, there will be tremendous destruction of the earth's habitat, and we once again see a key source of mankind's food reduced significantly. Mankind's ability to conduct commerce will also be curtailed.

Third Trumpet
WATER STRUCK

> "The third angel blew his trumpet, and a great star fell from heaven, blazing like a torch, and it fell on a third of the rivers and on the springs of water. The name of the star is Wormwood. A third of the waters became wormwood, and many people died from the water, because it had been made bitter" (Rev. 8:10-11).

The third trumpet releases a great star falling from heaven on the world's fresh water sources. This causes contamination of one-third of the world's drinking water. Mankind is now experiencing not only distress from the lack of food, but also thirst as God removes even the basics of life as part of his continued call for mankind to seek him.

Fourth Trumpet
LIGHT STRUCK

> "The fourth angel blew his trumpet, and a third of the sun was struck, and a third of the moon, and a third of the stars, so that a third of their light might be darkened, and a third of the day might be kept from shining, and likewise a third of the night" (Rev. 8:12).

The fourth trumpet extinguishes one-third of all natural light sources. As a result, light penetrating the atmosphere will be screened by one-third, severely curtailing photosynthesis. Again, the food chain is disrupted, while the physical darkness symbolically foreshadows the coming three woes of spiritual darkness.

Fifth through Seventh Trumpets
THE THREE WOES: SATANIC FORCES ON EARTH

> "Then I looked, and I heard an eagle crying with a loud voice as it flew directly overhead, "Woe, woe, woe to those who dwell

on the earth, at the blasts of the other trumpets that the three angels are about to blow!" (Rev. 8:13).

Once the events of the fourth trumpet come to conclusion, a warning goes out that signals a shift in focus. This shift is from God's direct causation of these end-times catastrophes to God's allowance of these events to be initiated by the forces of Satan through the release of demons on the earth. These demons initiate increasingly intense attacks directly on mankind. Scripture refers to these events as "the three woes."

The three woes appear to have organization, so we must ask what this organization means. As we look closely, we see that the pattern is related to the origin of each woe and how each increases in intensity over time.

The woes begin at the fifth trumpet. Their origin is *below the earth* with the release of the locusts from the bottomless pit. This escalates during the sixth trumpet, with the crossing of the Euphrates by the demonic army *(the surface of the earth)*. The seventh trumpet signals the fall of Satan to earth *(from heaven to earth)*. The gathering of these demonic forces as described in Revelation 18:2 is in preparation for their judgment and destruction. Unfortunately for the inhabitants of the earth, the presence of the entire host of demons throughout creation concentrated on earth makes life intolerable.

Fifth Trumpet
FIRST WOE

"And the fifth angel blew his trumpet, and I saw a star fallen from heaven to earth, and he was given the key to the shaft of the bottomless pit. He opened the shaft of the bottomless pit, and from the shaft rose smoke like the smoke of a great furnace, and the sun and the air were darkened with the smoke from the shaft. Then from the smoke came locusts on the earth, and they were given power like the power of scorpions of the earth. They were told not to harm the grass of the earth or any green plant or any tree, but only those people who do not have the seal of God on their foreheads. They were allowed to torment them for five months, but not to kill them, and their torment was like the torment of a scorpion when it stings someone. And in those days people will seek death and will not find it. They will long to die, but death will flee from them. In appearance the locusts were like horses prepared for battle: on their heads were what looked like crowns of gold; their faces were like human faces, their hair like women's hair, and their teeth like lions' teeth; they had breastplates like breastplates of iron, and the noise of their wings was like the noise of many chariots with horses rushing into battle. They have tails and stings like scorpions, and their power to hurt people for five months is in their tails. They have as king over them the angel of the bottomless pit. His name in Hebrew is Abaddon, and in Greek he is called Apollyon. The first woe has passed; behold, two woes are still to come" (Rev. 9:1-12).

The fifth trumpet brings the first woe, the opening of the bottomless pit. Here we see the shift in focus. During the seals and the first four trumpets, the focus is on the physical realm. From the fifth trumpet on, the focus shifts to the spiritual realm. We recognize this shift through the use of symbolic language, such as the use of a personal pronoun "he" to describe the star falling from heaven. Thus, these terrifying creatures are most likely fallen angels. This fallen angel opens the bottomless pit and releases another fallen angel that leads an army of creatures in attacking unrepentant mankind. We may also speculate that these are those mentioned in the book of Jude:

"And the angels who did not stay within their own position of authority, but left their proper dwelling, he has kept in eternal chains under gloomy darkness until the judgment of the great day" (Jude 1:6).

It is also at this time that we likely see the actual fulfillment of this prophecy, which speaks of the release of these fallen angels. Once kept in gloomy darkness, the fallen angels are released as judgment on unrepentant mankind at the great day of the Lord (see Appendix B). According to this account, these fallen angels take the form of creatures that resemble locusts.

We see locusts in Joel 1, as well:

"What the cutting locust left,
    the swarming locust has eaten.
What the swarming locust left,
    the hopping locust has eaten,
and what the hopping locust left,
    the destroying locust has eaten.

Awake, you drunkards, and weep,
    and wail, all you drinkers of wine,
because of the sweet wine,
    for it is cut off from your mouth.
For a nation has come up against my land,
    powerful and beyond number;
its teeth are lions' teeth,
    and it has the fangs of a lioness.
It has laid waste my vine
    and splintered my fig tree" (Joel 1: 4-7).

As in Revelation 9, the locusts of Joel 1 have the "teeth of lions" and swarm upon the land as part of the judgment of God. The similarity in the description to the fifth trumpet raises an interesting question. Can we take these events and overlay them? While on the surface it seems that we might, as we look closer, we see that these are actually different events. The creatures in Joel 1 destroy the vegetation. In Revelation 9, they are told not to harm the grass, green plants, or trees. Instead, they bite and torment people. This negates the possibility that they are describing the same event.

Sixth Trumpet
SECOND WOE

"Then the sixth angel blew his trumpet, and I heard a voice from
    the four horns of the golden altar before God, saying to the

sixth angel who had the trumpet, 'Release the four angels who are bound at the great river Euphrates.'

So the four angels, who had been prepared for the hour, the day, the month, and the year, were released to kill a third of mankind. The number of mounted troops was twice ten thousand times ten thousand; I heard their number. And this is how I saw the horses in my vision and those who rode them: they wore breastplates the color of fire and of sapphire and of sulfur, and the heads of the horses were like lions' heads, and fire and smoke and sulfur came out of their mouths. By these three plagues a third of mankind was killed, by the fire and smoke and sulfur coming out of their mouths. For the power of the horses is in their mouths and in their tails, for their tails are like serpents with heads, and by means of them they wound" (Rev. 9:13-19).

You would think that, with this level of suffering, the people of the earth would recognize that God's wrath is now against them and begin to repent. Not so. Even now, Revelation tells us that their hearts are so hardened that they do not.

"The rest of mankind, who were not killed by these plagues, did not repent of the works of their hands nor give up worshiping demons and idols of gold and silver and bronze and stone and wood, which cannot see or hear or walk, nor did they repent of their murders or their sorceries or their sexual immorality or their thefts" (Rev. 9:20-21).

Truly, God's upcoming unrestrained wrath is justified.

Also note that, in this second woe, we once again have demonic intervention. This time, however, demons originate from the earth's surface, the area of the Euphrates River. This is significant because in Genesis 15:18, God set the boundary of the land given to Abraham as the Euphrates. By crossing it, the army of the demons violates God's boundary. Despite this violation, God's mercy remains. He continues to restrain his wrath to one-third of his creation. This is the second woe.

The parallels between the second woe and the second chapter of Joel should not be missed. Beginning here, Joel 2 and 3 can be seen in the events of Revelation, leading up to and including the day of the Lord. The day of the Lord is a specific period at the end of the age.

> "Blow a trumpet in Zion; sound an alarm on my holy mountain! Let all the inhabitants of the land tremble, for the day of the Lord is coming; it is near, a day of darkness and gloom, a day of clouds and thick darkness! Like blackness there is spread upon the mountains a great and powerful people; their like has never been before, nor will be again after them through the years of all generations.
>
> Fire devours before them, and behind them a flame burns. The land is like the garden of Eden before them, but behind them a desolate wilderness, and nothing escapes them.
>
> Their appearance is like the appearance of horses, and like war horses they run. As with the rumbling of chariots, they leap on the tops of the mountains, like the crackling of a flame of fire devouring the stubble, like a powerful army drawn up for battle.
>
> Before them peoples are in anguish; all faces grow pale. Like warriors they charge; like soldiers they scale the wall. They march each on his way; they do not swerve from their paths. They do not jostle one another; each marches in his path; they burst through the weapons and are not halted. They leap upon the city, they run upon the walls, they climb up into the houses, they enter through the windows like a thief.
>
> The earth quakes before them; the heavens tremble. The sun and the moon are darkened, and the stars withdraw their shining. The Lord utters his voice before his army, for his camp is exceedingly great; he who executes his word is powerful. For the day of the Lord is great and very awesome; who can endure it?" (Joel 2:1-11).

This period of time is further explained in Appendix B.

ISRAEL'S CALL TO REPENTANCE

Even after all of these devastating events, the people of the earth still refuse to repent. This ultimately leads to God's final, inescapable judgment. But before that judgment falls, God sends forth one last call. The result is an ominous invitation to Israel that signals not only a warning, but yet another shift in focus in the book of Revelation—from a focus on the people of the earth generally, to a focus on Israel specifically. That focus remains through the rest of the book.

"Then I saw another mighty angel coming down from heaven, wrapped in a cloud, with a rainbow over his head, and his face was like the sun, and his legs like pillars of fire. He had a little scroll open in his hand. And he set his right foot on the sea, and his left foot on the land, and called out with a loud voice, like a lion roaring. When he called out, the seven thunders sounded.

And when the seven thunders had sounded, I was about to write, but I heard a voice from heaven saying, 'Seal up what the seven thunders have said, and do not write it down.'

And the angel whom I saw standing on the sea and on the land raised his right hand to heaven and swore by him who lives forever and ever, who created heaven and what is in it, the earth and what is in it, and the sea and what is in it, that there would be no more delay, but that in the days of the trumpet call to be sounded by the seventh angel, the mystery of God would be fulfilled, just as he announced to his servants the prophets.

Then the voice that I had heard from heaven spoke to me again, saying, 'Go, take the scroll that is open in the hand of the angel who is standing on the sea and on the land.' So I went to the angel and told him to give me the little scroll. And he said to me, 'Take and eat it; it will make your stomach bitter, but in your mouth it will be sweet as honey.' And I took the little scroll from the hand of the angel and ate it. It was sweet as honey in my mouth, but when I had eaten it my stomach was made bitter. And I was told,

'You must again prophesy about many peoples and nations and languages and kings'" (Rev. 10:1-11).

Although the meaning of this scroll is intentionally veiled, it is difficult to miss the similarities between Ezekiel's call as Israel's watchman (Eze. 3:1-9):

> "And he said to me, 'Son of man, eat whatever you find here. Eat this scroll, and go, speak to the house of Israel.' So I opened my mouth, and he gave me this scroll to eat. And he said to me, 'Son of man, feed your belly with this scroll that I give you and fill your stomach with it.' Then I ate it, and it was in my mouth as sweet as honey. And he said to me, 'Son of man, go to the house of Israel and speak with my words to them. For you are not sent to a people of foreign speech and a hard language, but to the house of Israel—not to many peoples of foreign speech and a hard language, whose words you cannot understand. Surely, if I sent you to such, they would listen to you. But the house of Israel will not be willing to listen to you, for they are not willing to listen to me: because all the house of Israel have a hard forehead and a stubborn heart. Behold, I have made your face as hard as their faces, and your forehead as hard as their foreheads. Like emery harder than flint have I made your forehead. Fear them not, nor be dismayed at their looks, for they are a rebellious house'" (Eze. 3:1-9).

This suggests that the seven thunders at the sixth trumpet could possibly serve as a specific call for Israel's repentance (sweet in the mouth) that will go unheeded (sour in the stomach). Since this call is specifically to Israel, the details are not to be revealed by John. Indeed, as we will see in subsequent chapters of Revelation, despite having been "consumed" (Jer. 5:3) by these events, Israel's faithlessness continues. Yet even now, God extends mercy and offers the opportunity to repent.

> "'Yet even now,' declares the Lord, 'return to me with all your heart, with fasting, with weeping, and with mourning; and

rend your hearts and not your garments.' Return to the Lord your God, for he is gracious and merciful, slow to anger, and abounding in steadfast love; and he relents over disaster. Who knows whether he will not turn and relent, and leave a blessing behind him, a grain offering and a drink offering for the Lord your God?" (Joel 2:12-14).

"Return, faithless Israel, declares the Lord. I will not look on you in anger, for I am merciful, declares the Lord; I will not be angry forever. Only acknowledge your guilt, that you rebelled against the Lord your God and scattered your favors among foreigners under every green tree, and that you have not obeyed my voice, declares the Lord" (Jer. 3:11-13).

"O Lord, do not your eyes look for truth? You have struck them down, but they felt no anguish; you have consumed them, but they refused to take correction. They have made their faces harder than rock; they have refused to repent" (Jer. 5:3).

If only Israel were to heed! The Bible is replete with examples of God's longsuffering toward his people and his aversion to punishing them. Yet, at this point, Israel is now at her greatest crossroads since her crucifixion of her Savior. This refusal to repent prepares the way for her acceptance of the Antichrist as her messiah and, consequently, the commencement of Daniel's Seventieth Week. The final seven-year tribulation period of Israel begins here at the sixth trumpet.

chapter five

DANIEL'S SEVENTIETH WEEK BEGINS

Then I was given a measuring rod like a staff, and I was told, "Rise and measure the temple of God and the altar and those who worship there, but do not measure the court outside the temple; leave that out, for it is given over to the nations, and they will trample the holy city for forty-two months. And I will grant authority to my two witnesses, and they will prophesy for 1,260 days, clothed in sackcloth.

These are the two olive trees and the two lampstands that stand before the Lord of the earth. And if anyone would harm them, fire pours from their mouth and consumes their foes. If anyone would harm them, this is how he is doomed to be killed. They have the power to shut the sky, that no rain may fall during the days of their prophesying, and they have power over the waters to turn them into blood and to strike the earth with every kind of plague, as often as they desire.

And when they have finished their testimony, the beast that rises from the bottomless pit will make war on them and conquer them and kill them, and their dead bodies will lie in the street of the great city that symbolically is called Sodom and Egypt, where their Lord was crucified. For three and a half days some from the peoples and tribes and languages and nations will gaze at their dead bodies and refuse to let them be placed in a tomb, and those who dwell on the earth will rejoice over them and make merry and exchange presents, because these two prophets had been a torment to those who dwell on the earth.

But after the three and a half days a breath of life from God entered them, and they stood up on their feet, and great fear fell on those who saw them. Then they heard a loud voice from heaven saying to them, "Come up here!" And they went up to heaven in a cloud, and their enemies watched them. And at that hour there was a great earthquake, and a tenth of the city fell. Seven thousand people were killed in the earthquake, and the rest were terrified and gave glory to the God of heaven.

The second woe has passed; behold, the third woe is soon to come.

REVELATION 11:1-14

This passage continues the focus on Israel that began in Revelation 10:11. We know this prophecy relates to Israel for three reasons. First, it flows from the discussion in the previous chapter. Second, we encounter our first reference to the third temple, which will be re-built prior to the Seventieth Week. Third, when we consider the verses about the three-and-one-half years, we see this tying into specific time references first prophesied in Daniel, which also focuses on Israel.

Indeed, the first section of Revelation 11 draws heavily on the book of Daniel. Therefore, to make sense of what is happening, let us look at the first of Daniel's visions of the key players and events:

"I considered the horns, and behold, there came up among them another horn, a little one, before which three of the first horns were plucked up by the roots. And behold, in this horn were eyes like the eyes of a man, and a mouth speaking great things" (Dan. 7:8).

Several verses later, an angel brings more detail to the prophecy by adding: "He [the king being described here] shall be different from the former ones, and shall put down three kings" (Dan. 7:24).

Two years later, Daniel was given another vision of the same "horn":

"Out of one of them came a little horn, which grew exceedingly great toward the south, toward the east, and toward the glorious land. It grew great, even to the host of heaven. And some of the host and some of the stars it threw down to the ground and trampled on them. It became great, even as great as the Prince of the host. And the regular burnt offering was taken away from him, and the place of his sanctuary was overthrown. And a host will be given over to it together with the regular burnt offering because of transgression, and it will throw truth to the ground, and it will act and prosper. Then I heard a holy one speaking, and another holy one said to the one who spoke, 'For how long is the vision concerning the regular burnt offering, the transgression that makes desolate, and the giving over of the sanctuary and host to be trampled underfoot?' And he said to me, 'For 2,300 evenings and mornings. Then the sanctuary shall be restored to its rightful state'" (Dan. 8:9-14).

The angel Gabriel provides the interpretation of this prophecy. He does so in two different places: Daniel 8–9, and Daniel 11.

"And at the latter end of their kingdom, when the transgressors have reached their limit, a king of bold face, one who understands riddles, shall arise. His power shall be great—but not by his own power; and he shall cause fearful destruction and shall succeed in what he does, and destroy mighty men and the people who are the saints. By his cunning he shall make deceit prosper under his hand, and in his own mind he shall become great. Without warning he shall destroy many" (Dan. 8:23-25).

"And the people of the prince who is to come shall destroy the city and the sanctuary. Its end shall come with a flood, and to the end there shall be war. Desolations are decreed. And he shall make a strong covenant with many for one week, and for half of the week he shall put an end to sacrifice and offering" (Dan. 9:26-27).

"Forces from him shall appear and profane the temple and fortress and shall take away the regular burnt offering" (Dan. 11:31).

Remember, in Revelation 10 John is told that despite God's gracious offer of mercy (the little book being sweet in his mouth), Israel will reject God's call to repentance (the little book growing sour in John's stomach). In doing so, Israel triggers Daniel's Seventieth Week, the seven-year time period that concludes the Seventy Weeks prophecy given to Daniel more than two thousand years earlier. (For details on the Seventieth Week, see Appendix A.) By overlaying all the information given to us in Revelation and Daniel, we can develop a timeline for this period. (See "Daniel's Seventieth Week" chart.) These references also speak directly to the character and events surrounding Israel's false messiah, with whom Israel makes this covenant. This false messiah is known by many names, including the Antichrist. (See "Daniel Characters in Revelation" chart.)

DANIEL'S FOURTH BEAST (THE BEAST OUT OF THE SEA)
(Second, Fourth and Fifth Heads Fall) (Sixth Head Takes Power)

With Israel's refusal to repent, the stage is set for her acceptance of the Antichrist. This occurs at the beginning of Daniel's Seventieth Week as described in Daniel 9 (see Appendix A) and Daniel 11:31. This passage describes events in Jerusalem during the first half (or three-and-one-half years) of this seven-year period. Israel's acceptance of this false messiah comes in the form of a covenant that transfers temple worship to him (Dan. 8:11-14, 9:27).

"It [the horn] became great, even as great as the Prince of the host. And the regular burnt offering was taken away from him, and the place of his sanctuary was overthrown. And a host will be given over to it together with the regular burnt offering

DANIEL'S 70TH WEEK — 6th Trumpet Through 7th Bowl of Revelation

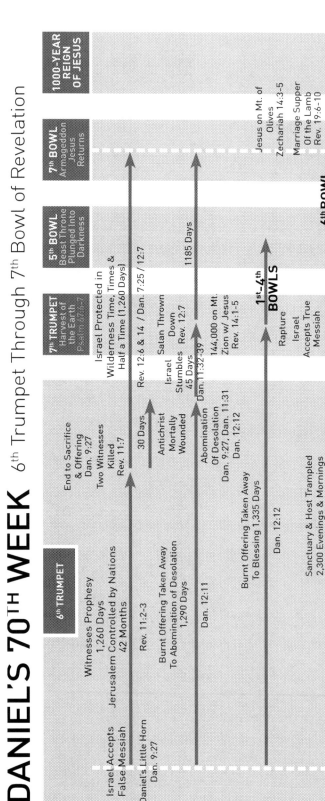

DANIEL CHARACTERS in Revelation

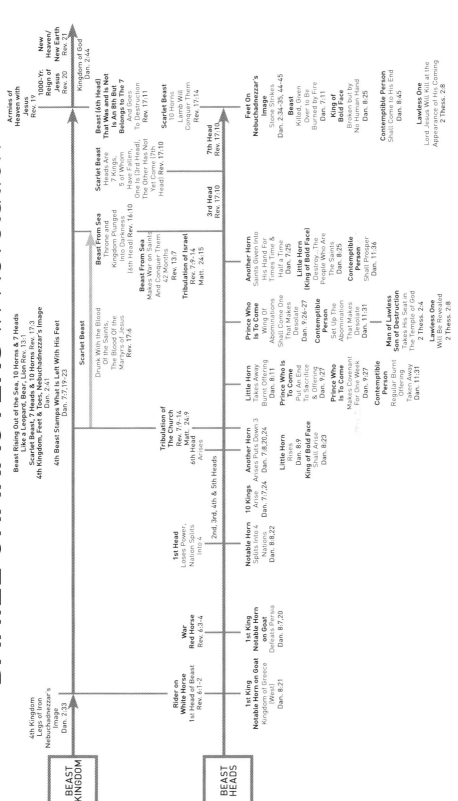

BEAST KINGDOM

4th Kingdom
Legs of Iron
Nebuchadnezzar's
Image
Dan. 2:33

Rider on White Horse
1st Head of Beast
Rev. 6:1-2

War Red Horse
Rev. 6:3-4

1st Head
Loses Power,
Nation Splits
Into 4

2nd, 3rd, 4th & 5th Heads

Tribulation of The Church
Rev. 7:9-14
Matt. 24:9
6th Head
Arises

Scarlet Beast

Drunk With the Blood Of the Saints,
The Blood Of the
Martyrs of Jesus
Rev. 17:6

Beast From Sea
Throne and
Kingdom Plunged
Into Darkness
(6th Head) Rev. 16:10

Beast From Sea
Makes War on Saints
And Conquer Them
42 Months
Rev. 13:7

Tribulation of Israel
Rev. 7:9-14
Matt. 24:15

Scarlet Beast
Heads Are
7 Kings,
5 of Whom
Have Fallen,
One Is (3rd Head),
The Other Has Not
Yet Come (7th
Head) Rev. 17:10

**Beast (6th Head)
That Was and Is Not
Is An 8th But
Belongs to The 7**
And Goes
To Destruction
Rev. 17:11

Scarlet Beast
10 Horns
Lamb Will
Conquer Them
Rev. 17:14

Armies of Heaven with Jesus
Rev. 19

1000-Yr. Reign of Jesus
Rev. 20

New Heaven/ New Earth
Rev. 21

Kingdom of God
Dan. 2:44

Beast Rising Out of the Sea, 10 Horns & 7 Heads
Like a Leopard, Bear, Lion Rev. 13:1
Scarlet Beast, 7 Heads & 10 Horns Rev. 17:3
4th Kingdom, Feet & Toes, Nebuchadnezzar's Image
Dan. 2:41

4th Beast Stamps What Is Left With His Feet
Dan. 7:7,19-23

BEAST HEADS

**1st King
Notable Horn on Goat**
Kingdom of Greece
(West)
Dan. 8:21

**1st King
Notable Horn
on Goat**
Defeats Persia
Dan. 8:7,20

Notable Horn
Splits Into 4
Nations
Dan. 8:8,22

10 Kings
Arise
Dan. 7:7,24

Another Horn
Arises Puts Down 3
Dan. 7:8,20,24

Little Horn
Rises
Dan. 8:9

King of Bold Face
Shall Arise
Dan. 8:23

Little Horn
Takes Away
Burnt Offering
Dan. 8:11

**Prince Who Is
To Come**
Put An End
To Sacrifice
& Offering
Dan. 9:27

**Prince Who
Is To Come**
Makes Covenant
For One Week
Dan. 9:27

**Contemptible
Person**
Regular Burnt
Offering
Taken Away
Dan. 11:31

**Prince Who
Is To Come**
Wing Of
Abominations
Shall Come One
That Makes
Desolate
Dan. 9:26-27

**Contemptible
Person**
Set Up The
Abomination
That Makes
Desolate
Dan. 11:31

**Man of Lawless
Son of Destruction**
Takes His Seat in
The Temple of God
2 Thess. 2:4

Lawless One
Will Be Revealed
2 Thess. 2:8

Another Horn
Saints Given Into
His Hand For
Times Time &
Half a Time
Dan. 7:25

**Little Horn
(King of Bold Face)**
Destroy...The
People Who Are
The Saints
Dan. 8:25

**Contemptible
Person**
Shall Prosper
Dan. 11:36

3rd Head
Rev. 17:10

7th Head
Rev. 17:10

**Feet On
Nebuchadnezzar's
Image**
Stone Strikes
Dan. 2:34-35, 44-45

Beast
Killed, Given
Over to Be
Burned by Fire
Dan. 7:11

**King of
Bold Face**
Broken but by
No Human Hand
Dan. 8:25

Contemptible Person
Shall Come to His End
Dan. 8:45

Lawless One
Lord Jesus Will Kill at the
Appearance of His Coming
2 Thess. 2:8

because of transgression, and it will throw truth to the ground, and it will act and prosper" (Dan. 8:11-12).

This person, the Antichrist, is the little horn of Daniel's fourth beast (Daniel 7:7-8) and the sixth head of the scarlet beast (Rev. 17:10; also seen in Revelation 13:1 as the beast from the sea). After the events of the third seal, the Antichrist takes power from three other horns (or national leaders, Dan. 7:8, 7:24). If the notable horn (in nation form) is the United States, then the four heads of the beast kingdom represent four regional governments (nations), each with authority after the breakup of the United States. The Re-United States of America (the beast nation), therefore, represents the consolidation of power from three quarters of these regional governments into one central authority led by the Antichrist.

It is worth noting that "the beast" here is spoken of both as a person and a government. This is due to the nature and character of the beast, who likely plays a role in this government throughout its entire existence and whose character infuses it. As such, the beast and the nation he leads are indistinguishable in their nature and purpose. Although the person (the Antichrist) remains the same, the government of which he is a part changes through time, as do its leaders (or heads).

To review, the Antichrist is likely present behind the scenes as the first head takes power at the opening of the first seal. He then assumes power of one of the four regions after the United States splits into four regional governments. The destruction of three of the national leaders ("heads") causes the re-uniting of three quarters of the United States under his dictatorial authority. The Antichrist then pursues and obtains a protective covenant with Israel, commencing Daniel's Seventieth Week.

By Israel's joining in covenant with the Antichrist for protection, she accepts him as messiah, thus transferring (taking away) the sacrifice of the regular burnt offering from God to him (Dan 8:11, 11:31). By accepting this covenant, Israel fulfills Jesus' prediction in John 5:43: "I have come in my Father's name, and you do not receive me. If another comes in his own name, you will receive him."

Zechariah also prophesied concerning the rejection of Christ, the

Good Shepherd, and Israel's acceptance of the "foolish shepherd." We find rejection of this Good Shepherd prophesied in Zechariah 11:9-14:

> "So I said, 'I will not be your shepherd. What is to die, let it die. What is to be destroyed, let it be destroyed. And let those who are left devour the flesh of one another.' And I took my staff Favor, and I broke it, annulling the covenant that I had made with all the peoples. So it was annulled on that day, and the sheep traders, who were watching me, knew that it was the word of the Lord. Then I said to them, 'If it seems good to you, give me my wages; but if not, keep them.' And they weighed out as my wages thirty pieces of silver. Then the Lord said to me, 'Throw it to the potter'—the lordly price at which I was priced by them. So I took the thirty pieces of silver and threw them into the house of the Lord, to the potter. Then I broke my second staff, Union, annulling the brotherhood between Judah and Israel."

Immediately following in verses 15-17, Zechariah describes the acceptance of the foolish one:

> "Then the Lord said to me, 'Take once more the equipment of a foolish shepherd. For behold, I am raising up in the land a shepherd who does not care for those being destroyed, or seek the young or heal the maimed or nourish the healthy, but devours the flesh of the fat ones, tearing off even their hoofs.
>
> 'Woe to my worthless shepherd,
>   who deserts the flock!
> May the sword strike his arm
>   and his right eye!
> Let his arm be wholly withered,
>   his right eye utterly blinded!'"

Israel's acceptance of this foolish shepherd occurs just prior to Zechariah's discussion of Jerusalem as a "cup of staggering" and his reference to the day of the Lord. So once again, we see the prophetic

Scripture confirming the chronology of Revelation. Between Israel's rejection of Christ and her acceptance of the foolish shepherd, we also see corroboration of the gap in time found between Daniel's sixty-ninth and Seventieth weeks.

THE LINEAGE OF THE ANTICHRIST

In order to be an acceptable "messiah," this Antichrist must be Jewish, descended from Abraham and David. The Messianic genealogy through Abraham begins in Genesis 12:1-3 and is confirmed in Genesis 22:18. The line through David is found in Psalm 132:11, Jeremiah 23:5-6, 33:15-16, and 2 Samuel 7:12-16. Based on Daniel 9:26, this person must also come from the people who destroyed the temple in 70 A.D., which is Rome (the West). Therefore, the Antichrist has an acceptable Messianic lineage but comes out of the West.

Unfortunately, there is nothing in the prophecies that would help us set the exact time of the Antichrist's emergence. We do know, however, that after the breakup of the beast nation and prior to reuniting it, the Antichrist forms the 10-nation alliance.

There is a second player in here, too. As we will see later in Revelation, that is the false prophet. Scripture describes the Antichrist and the false prophet as a satanic duo, with the Antichrist as the political arm and the false prophet as the spiritual one. With the martyrdom of the church completed at the sixth seal, the false prophet is the one leading the persecution. First introduced to us as the "beast from out of the earth (Rev. 13:11), but commonly called "the false prophet" because of his reference by this name in Revelation 19:20, he will head up what appears to be a one-world religion that severely persecutes the church. That is why the beast we eventually see in Revelation 17 is scarlet—it is drenched with the blood of the saints. The political beast is in power, but the spiritual element is driving the persecution.

One of the identifying features of the Antichrist is that he will take away the burnt offering. This tells us that at some point in the future, Israel must institute animal sacrifices. By extension, the temple must be rebuilt sometime before the Seventieth Week (Deut. 12:13-14), as well. The Scriptures appear to be silent on the timing and circumstances surrounding this reconstruction, but this and subsequent events imply its occurrence.

How will this all come about? Here is one possible scenario. During the first half of the week (or for three-and-one-half years) under this covenant, Jerusalem will be controlled by the nations. The covenant will include Israel ceding her defenses to the Antichrist and relinquishing her autonomy to the nations by placing her dependence on the Antichrist, not God. At this time, God sends the two witnesses as Israel's final call to repentance.

The identity of these witnesses remains speculative. However, I believe one will be Elijah. This is based on Malachi 4:5:

> "Behold, I will send you Elijah the prophet before the great and awesome day of the Lord comes. And he will turn the hearts of fathers to their children and the hearts of children to their fathers, lest I come and strike the land with a decree of utter destruction" (Mal. 4:5-6).

The emergence of the two witnesses occurs immediately before the day of the Lord, which begins at the blowing of the seventh trumpet. Therefore, it is reasonable to see one of these two witnesses as Elijah. Just as John the Baptist called for Israel's repentance at Jesus' first advent and is considered a "type" of Elijah (Mark 9:13), here in Revelation 11, Elijah *himself* calls for Israel's repentance just prior to Jesus' second advent. Once again, Israel's call to repentance will be rejected.

Elijah is a likely candidate for this witness because there are only two people in the Scriptures described as not having experienced death at the end of their recorded lives. The first is Elijah, who was taken up in a whirlwind (2 Kings 2:11). The second is Enoch, who "was not because God had taken him" (Heb. 11:5). Enoch, therefore, is likely the other witness. If Elijah and Enoch are the two end-times witnesses, this would give us witnesses from both the ante- and post-diluvian periods.

chapter six

SEVENTH TRUMPET THE DAY OF THE LORD BEGINS

THE KINGDOM OF THE WORLD BECOMES THE KINGDOM OF OUR LORD

Then the seventh angel blew his trumpet, and there were loud voices in heaven, saying, "The kingdom of the world has become the kingdom of our Lord and of his Christ, and he shall reign forever and ever." And the twenty-four elders who sit on their thrones before God fell on their faces and worshiped God, saying, "We give thanks to you, Lord God Almighty, who is and who was, for you have taken your great power and begun to reign. The nations raged, but your wrath came, and the time for the dead to be judged, and for rewarding your servants, the prophets and saints, and those who fear your name, both small and great, and for destroying the destroyers of the earth." Then God's temple in heaven was opened, and the ark of his covenant was seen within his temple. There were flashes of lightning, rumblings, peals of thunder, an earthquake, and heavy hail.

REVELATION 11:15-19

The blowing of the seventh trumpet commences the day of the Lord, a period of time during which Jesus re-establishes his authority over all creation. (See Appendix B.) Although this passage tells us that Jesus has begun to reign, that reign is established incrementally. It starts here in the final half of Daniel's Seventieth Week and extends through his millennial reign to the final judgment (Rev. 20:11-15). This allows additional time for repentance and the fulfillment of all God's promises to Israel.

This is a terrifying, exciting, and powerful time because it is also the time of final harvest. As we will discuss over the next several chapters, this harvest occurs in two phases: the grain harvest (the harvest of the righteous) and the grape harvest (the harvest of the wicked). The harvest of the righteous includes the rapture of the followers of Christ and the national salvation of Israel (although Israel is not taken in the rapture but is protected through the day of the Lord). This is followed by the destruction of the wicked during the bowl judgments when God's full, unrestrained wrath is poured out.

How do we know that the rapture occurs during the blowing of the seventh trumpet? There are some very clear Scriptural indicators.

1. From the prophecies of Daniel, we know that the coming of God's eternal kingdom is the time of final judgment.

2. In Revelation 11:15, the angel declares that the time has come for the kingdoms of the world to become those of Jesus Christ. Therefore Revelation 11:15 is the coming of God's eternal kingdom and the time of final judgment.

3. The coming of Jesus to reap (and judge) the earth is preceded by the blowing of the last and final trumpet (1 Cor. 15:51-52). The seventh trumpet is the last and final trumpet.

4. The final trumpet and the coming of Christ also precede the national salvation of Israel. This also occurs at the seventh trumpet.

The description of the rapture itself is not given to us during the description of the seventh trumpet. It is saved for a theological interlude that immediately follows in Revelation 12 and 13, where John provides much of the historical background and detail not provided in the main chronology. Instead, here at the seventh trumpet John uses the broader imagery of the harvest.

Harvest imagery is used throughout the Scriptures as one of the characteristics of the end times. Most people will remember it from Jesus' words in Mark 4:

> "He also said, 'This is what the kingdom of God is like. A man scatters seed on the ground. Night and day, whether he sleeps or gets up, the seed sprouts and grows, though he does not know how. All by itself the soil produces grain—first the stalk, then the head, then the full kernel in the head. As soon as the grain is ripe, he puts the sickle to it, because the harvest has come'" (Mark 4:26-29).

In this parable, the kingdom of God is compared to a seed placed in the soil that produces grain and is harvested with a sickle when ripe. Now at the seventh trumpet, that harvest begins. As it does, the kingdom of our Lord consumes the kingdoms of the world.

chapter seven

FIRST THEOLOGICAL INTERLUDE

INTRODUCTION TO THE FIRST THEOLOGICAL INTERLUDE

We now enter a section of Revelation in which the narrative is interrupted by two theological interludes. The first spans Revelation chapters 12–13. The second spans Revelation 17–18. These interludes are designed to provide the reader with historical context that helps them understand more about the individuals and symbols involved during this time. In these sections, we see the characters represented as symbols, even though the events themselves are literal.

In the first interlude, Revelation 12–13, we gain background specific to the seventh trumpet and all the events that surround it. In Revelation 11:15, we read the description of the blowing of the seventh trumpet that precedes God's wrath. In Revelation 12, we are given background that sets the stage why God's wrath must be poured out unrestrained from this point on. In Revelation 13, we are given details on what is happening on earth at the time the seventh trumpet is actually blown.

The blowing of the seventh trumpet is the point in the chronology at which we shift from Satan's control of this world to God's. Even though God is ultimately sovereign over the universe, he has allowed Satan to have authority over the world system for a time. Evil is allowed and even used for refinement and to bring people into the kingdom. However, it is at this point that this control will be systematically taken away until God's kingdom begins its total control of the world system at Christ's return.

This is why the information on the spiritual and historical context is placed here. This interlude pauses the chronology; were we to pull out these two chapters we would still have a continuous flow from the blowing of the seventh trumpet through Revelation 14. Beyond Revelation 14, the chronology continues to the second interlude at Revelation 17–18, then resumes without interruption to the end.

THE GREAT SIGNS IN HEAVEN

Revelation 12 opens with important historical background for understanding the seventh and final trumpet. John introduces this section with the sign of the woman:

> "And a great sign appeared in heaven: a woman clothed with the sun, with the moon under her feet, and on her head a crown of twelve stars. She was pregnant and was crying out in birth pains and the agony of giving birth" (Rev. 12:1-2).

In this vision, the woman represents Israel in the first century. Having been given intimate knowledge of God, Israel is preparing the world for the advent of Jesus on earth. This prophecy was fulfilled in history past. The vision includes references to the sun, moon, and twelve stars, which represent Jacob (the sun), Rachel (the moon), and the twelve brothers (including Joseph). In other words, together they represent the entire house of Israel (Gen. 37:9-10).

> "And another sign appeared in heaven: behold, a great red dragon, with seven heads and ten horns, and on his heads seven diadems. His tail swept down a third of the stars of heaven and cast them to the earth. And the dragon stood before the woman who was about to give birth, so that when she bore her child he might devour it" (Rev. 12:3-4).

In the second sign, we see a dragon, identified in Revelation 12:9 as Satan, casting one-third of the angels to earth. His goal was to prevent Jesus' advent. This was also fulfilled in history past.

> "She gave birth to a male child, one who is to rule all the nations with a rod of iron, but her child was caught up to God and to his throne" (Rev. 12:5).

In the third sign, we see the birth of Jesus. Despite Satan's best efforts, Jesus is born into the world and obtains his authority over the nations through his sacrifice on the cross. In this prophecy, we see Jesus ascended to God's throne and seated at the right hand of the Father (cf. Mark 16:19). This prophecy was also fulfilled in history past. Jesus' rule with a rod of iron is yet future.

With this background, we now move into yet unfulfilled prophecy and return to the events unfolding at the time of the seventh trumpet. In this fourth sign, we see Israel's flight into the wilderness and protection during the outpouring of God's unrestrained wrath.

> "And the woman fled into the wilderness, where she has a place prepared by God, in which she is to be nourished for 1,260 days" (Rev. 12:6).

Why does Israel flee? In Revelation 13, we are told that the false prophet (or "the beast from the earth," Rev.13:11-18) places an image of the Antichrist in the Holy of Holies to be worshipped (vv. 14-15; cf. Matt. 24:15-28). This abomination is set up 1290 days (or thirty days beyond the three-and-one-half-year midpoint of Daniel's Seventieth Week) after the burnt offering is taken away (Dan. 11:31-45; 12:11). Although Israel initially accepts the Antichrist as her messiah, the abomination of desolation reveals the Antichrist's true nature and breaks the covenant between them. The Antichrist reveals himself as a false messiah by declaring himself to be God (or in place of God) and begins his relentless persecution of Israel.

> "And they shall set up the abomination that makes desolate....
> And the king shall do as he wills. He shall exalt himself and

magnify himself above every god, and shall speak astonishing things against the God of gods. He shall prosper till the indignation is accomplished; for what is decreed shall be done. He shall pay no attention to the gods of his fathers, or to the one beloved by women. He shall not pay attention to any other god, for he shall magnify himself above all. He shall honor the god of fortresses instead of these" (Dan. 11:31-37).

"And from the time that the regular burnt offering is taken away and the abomination that makes desolate is set up, there shall be 1,290 days" (Dan. 12:11).

The timing and sequence of the setting up of the abomination of desolation is so significant that Jesus describes it in detail in three of the four gospels:

"So when you see the abomination of desolation spoken of by the prophet Daniel, standing in the holy place (let the reader understand), then let those who are in Judea flee to the mountains. Let the one who is on the housetop not go down to take what is in his house, and let the one who is in the field not turn back to take his cloak. And alas for women who are pregnant and for those who are nursing infants in those days! Pray that your flight may not be in winter or on a Sabbath. For then there will be great tribulation, such as has not been from the beginning of the world until now, no, and never will be. And if those days had not been cut short, no human being would be saved. But for the sake of the elect those days will be cut short" (Matt. 24:15-22).

"But when you see the abomination of desolation standing where he ought not to be (let the reader understand), then let those who are in Judea flee to the mountains. Let the one who is on the housetop not go down, nor enter his house, to take anything out, and let the one who is in the field not turn back to take his cloak. And alas for women who are pregnant and for those who are nursing infants in those days! Pray that it may not happen in winter. For in those days there will be such tribulation as has not been from the beginning of the creation that God created until now, and never will be. And if the Lord had not cut short the days, no human being would be saved. But for the sake of the elect, whom he chose, he shortened the days" (Mark 13:14-20).

"But when you see Jerusalem surrounded by armies, then know that its desolation has come near. Then let those who are in Judea flee to the mountains, and let those who are inside the city depart, and let not those who are out in the country enter it, for these are days of vengeance, to fulfill all that is written. Alas for women who are pregnant and for those who are nursing infants in those days! For there will be great distress upon the earth and wrath against this people. They will fall by the edge of the sword and be led captive among all nations, and Jerusalem will be trampled underfoot by the Gentiles, until the times of the Gentiles are fulfilled" (Luke 21:20-24).

This abomination is also one of the signs given in 2 Thessalonians 2:3-4 that will occur prior to the day of the Lord.

"Let no one deceive you in any way. For that day [the day of the Lord] will not come, unless the rebellion comes first, and the man of lawlessness is revealed, the son of destruction, who opposes and exalts himself against every so-called god or object of worship, so that he takes his seat in the temple of God, proclaiming himself to be God."

WAR IN HEAVEN

Described next is the great war in heaven, with the Archangel Michael and his angels arrayed against Satan and his fallen angels. At this point, Satan is thrown out of heaven to the earth.

"Now war arose in heaven, Michael and his angels fighting against the dragon. And the dragon and his angels fought back, but he was defeated, and there was no longer any place for them in heaven. And the great dragon was thrown down, that ancient serpent, who is called the devil and Satan, the deceiver of the whole world—he was thrown down to the earth, and his angels were thrown down with him. And I heard a loud voice in heaven, saying, 'Now the salvation and the power and the kingdom of our God and the authority of his Christ have come, for the accuser of our brothers has been thrown down, who accuses them day and night before our God. And they have conquered him by the blood of the Lamb and by the word of their testimony, for they loved not their lives even unto death'" (Rev. 12:7-11).

This might strike many readers as strange because it occurs sometime in the future. Does this mean that, even today, Satan is occupying a place in heaven and will continue to do so until the end times? Yes. Zechariah 3:1 and Revelation 12:7-11 both indicate that Satan currently stands in heaven accusing the saints, both Old Testament and New Testament, before the throne of God.

At the seventh trumpet, when Jesus begins to exercise his authority and establish his reign, he eliminates evil from heaven by casting out both Satan and his angels. This is not to be confused with Satan's fall described in Luke 10:18. Satan, having previously lost his place of authority, now loses his place as accuser of the elect, as well. We see his fall and throwing down (cut down) described in Isaiah 14:12-14:

"How you are fallen from heaven,
    O Day Star, son of Dawn!
How you are cut down to the ground,
    you who laid the nations low!
You said in your heart,
    'I will ascend to heaven;
above the stars of God

I will set my throne on high;
I will sit on the mount of assembly
in the far reaches of the north;
I will ascend above the heights of the clouds;
I will make myself like the Most High.'"

SATAN LOSES POSITION

"On that day the Lord will punish
the host of heaven, in heaven,
and the kings of the earth, on the earth" (Isaiah 24:21).

Being thrown down from heaven is the first of three major changes in Satan's position at the time of the end. We see all of these detailed starting in Revelation 12:7–11. The second stage comes later, in Revelation 20:2-3, when Satan is thrown into the bottomless pit. The third change comes in Revelation 20:10 when Satan is thrown into the lake of fire. This culminates his progressive descent from his original position of authority (Luke 10:18).

The throwing down of Satan is an earth-shattering event. We see the power and gravity of this moment described in the synoptic gospels, as well. Jesus describes the start of this time period as shaking in the heavens with great and dramatic signs.

"Immediately after the tribulation of those days the sun will be darkened, and the moon will not give its light, and the stars will fall from heaven, and the powers of the heavens will be shaken" (Matt. 24:29).

"But in those days, after that tribulation, the sun will be darkened, and the moon will not give its light, and the stars will be falling from heaven, and the powers in the heavens will be shaken" (Mark 13:24-25).

"And there will be signs in sun and moon and stars, and on the earth distress of nations in perplexity because of the roaring of the sea and the waves, people fainting with fear and with foreboding of what is coming on the world. For the powers of the heavens will be shaken" (Luke 21:25-26).

This moment in history was also prophesied by Daniel:

"At that time shall arise Michael, the great prince who has charge of your people. And there shall be a time of trouble, such as never has been since there was a nation till that time" (Dan. 12:1).

Here we see Michael, Israel's angelic prince, precipitating an unprecedented time of trouble. We know this to be Israel's great tribulation.

THE THIRD WOE

At this point, the woes are coming to a close. It is time for the third woe, which will now be visited upon the earth in the form of Satan's earthly presence.

"Therefore, rejoice, O heavens and you who dwell in them! But *woe* to you, O earth and sea, for the devil has come down to you in great wrath, because he knows that his time is short!" (Rev. 12:12, emphasis mine).

The third woe has come. Satan's presence and wrath brings death and destruction at a level never seen before in history. It is in this earthly presence of Satan, combined with the vacuum of restraint created by the mass martyrdom of believers as a result of the seals and the imminent rapture, that we see evil completely unleashed. In this vacuum, it is no surprise that we see the culmination of power by the Antichrist. His coming is also seen in 2 Thessalonians 2:9, where he is called "the man of lawlessness." Elsewhere, he is described as being with "the activity of Satan," with power and false signs and wonders and wicked deception. That the Antichrist would be acting in accordance with "the activity of Satan" makes sense at this point since his rise to power coincides with the time that Satan is thrown down from heaven. This gives Satan the perfect opportunity to indwell the Antichrist and empower him to deceive. It is shortly following this time that the Antichrist receives his mortal wound and is healed (Rev. 13:3).

WAR ON EARTH: THE GREAT TRIBULATION OF ISRAEL

Following the war in heaven is a war on earth. At this point, we see that Satan has endowed the beast with authority to control mankind and attack the people of God. First—through the Antichrist—Satan attacks the original covenant people of God, Israel. Then he attacks the followers of Jesus.

> "And when the dragon saw that he had been thrown down to the earth, he pursued the woman who had given birth to the male child. But the woman was given the two wings of the great eagle so that she might fly from the serpent into the wilderness, to the place where she is to be nourished for a time, and times, and half a time. The serpent poured water like a river out of his mouth after the woman, to sweep her away with a flood. But the earth came to the help of the woman, and the earth opened its mouth and swallowed the river that the dragon had poured from his mouth. Then the dragon became furious with the woman and went off to make war on the rest of her offspring, on those who keep the commandments of God and hold to the testimony of Jesus" (Rev. 12:13-17).

Now embodied in the Antichrist, Satan's efforts are global (Rev. 12:13, 13:12). Through his puppet, the false prophet, he persecutes the followers of Jesus with a single-minded passion and ferocity. His efforts are focused on those who have been saved through the first five trumpets. Following the harvest of the earth, he pursues those not receiving the mark of the beast and thereby eliminates all followers of Jesus on earth.

What is happening with Israel during this time? Although Israel has yet to experience national repentance, God is preparing a remnant for salvation. He does this through the great tribulation of Israel, a time in which many are lost but the remnant receives divine protection (Rev. 12:14). This time of protection was foreseen by David and described in Psalm 124:1-8:

> "If it had not been the Lord who was on our side—
>   let Israel now say—
> if it had not been the Lord who was on our side
>   when people rose up against us,
> then they would have swallowed us up alive,
>   when their anger was kindled against us;
> then the flood would have swept us away,
>   the torrent would have gone over us;
> then over us would have gone
>   the raging waters.
> Blessed be the Lord,
> who has not given us
> as prey to their teeth!
> We have escaped like a bird
> from the snare of the fowlers;
> the snare is broken,
> and we have escaped!
> Our help is in the name of the Lord,
> who made heaven and earth."

How long does Israel's tribulation last? Although the violence is furious, it is limited. God has set a boundary. In Revelation, it is spelled out as 1,260 days or three-and-one-half years. In the parallel passages in Daniel, we see this described in the ancient Hebrew form "time, times, and half a time":

> "And someone said to the man clothed in linen, who was above the waters of the stream, 'How long shall it be till the end of these wonders?' And I heard the man clothed in linen, who was above the waters of the stream; he raised his right hand and his left hand toward heaven and swore by him who lives forever that it would be for a time, times, and half a time, and that when the shattering of the power of the holy people comes to an end all these things would be finished" (Dan. 12:6-7).

So that believers alive during this time will understand clearly what is happening, Daniel gives us additional information on the Antichrist and his activities. Daniel even gives us details of a battle plan laid out against him:

> "He [the Antichrist] shall deal with the strongest fortresses with the help of a foreign god. Those who acknowledge him he shall load with honor. He shall make them rulers over many and shall divide the land for a price. At the time of the end, the king of the south shall attack him, but the king of the north shall rush upon him like a whirlwind, with chariots and horsemen, and with many ships. And he shall come into countries and shall overflow and pass through. He shall come into the glorious land. And tens of thousands shall fall, but these shall be delivered out of his hand: Edom and Moab and the main part of the Ammonites. He shall stretch out his hand against the countries, and the land of Egypt shall not escape. He shall become ruler of the treasures of gold and of silver, and all the precious things of Egypt, and the Libyans and the Cushites shall follow in his train. But news from the east and the north shall alarm him, and he shall go out with great fury to destroy and devote many to destruction. And he shall pitch his palatial tents between the sea and the glorious holy mountain. Yet he shall come to his end, with none to help him" (Dan. 11:39-45).

The Antichrist will bring a level of destruction to Israel and the Middle East that will be incomprehensible, but his reign will not last forever. The Scriptures promise that "all Israel" shall be saved and that the Antichrist shall be destroyed.

> "And on the wing of abominations shall come one who makes desolate, until the decreed end is poured out on the desolator" (Dan. 9:27).

> "Alas! That day is so great there is none like it; it is a time of distress for Jacob; yet he shall be saved out of it" (Jer. 30:7).

WORLD GOVERNMENT
Beast out of the Sea

The great persecution by Satan will ultimately come to an end. However, we can tell both from this theological interlude and from the main chronological narrative that until that time, there is the appearance that evil is prevailing. For the benefit of those still alive during this time, Scripture provides us with a description of the kingdom (or in modern language, nation) and ultimately the international alliance that he leads. We are given this information so that believers can find peace in knowing that all of these events are foreknown by God and under his sovereign control.

What does Scripture tell us about the nation led by the Antichrist? By putting together Daniel 2, Daniel 7, and Revelation 17, we learn that throughout the time of the end, there will be a "beast nation" that, over time, has seven heads (or national leaders) that we have been discussing. One of these leaders, the sixth head, will be the Antichrist. One by one, all of these leaders move this kingdom toward participation in the 10-nation alliance. Although this alliance likely forms back when the four heads are in power, it does not gain full strength until the seventh trumpet under control of the Antichrist.

Although all of the leaders of the beast nation will move the kingdom toward global power, it is only here, with the mark of the beast in Revelation 13, that we see that power coming to reality:

> "And I saw a beast rising out of the sea, with ten horns and seven heads, with ten diadems on its horns and blasphemous names on its heads. And the beast that I saw was like a leopard; its feet were like a bear's, and its mouth was like a lion's mouth. And to it the dragon gave his power and his throne and great authority. One of its heads seemed to have a mortal wound, but its mortal wound was healed, *and the whole earth marveled as they followed the beast.* And they worshiped the dragon, for he had given his authority to the beast, and they worshiped the

beast, saying, 'Who is like the beast, and who can fight against it?'" (Rev. 13:1-4, emphasis mine).

At this point in the chronology, four of the heads (or national leaders) of the beast nation have risen and fallen. At the end of the seventh trumpet, the Antichrist (the sixth head) is in power. A graphical illustration of the beast kingdom as it changes throughout the time of the end can be found in the charts "The Beast through the Time of the End" and "The Beast of Revelation."

To this point, we have seen six of the seven heads having held power, with one yet to come. Once the mortal head wound of the sixth head, the Antichrist, is healed by the power of Satan, he is legitimized as an object of worship led by the false prophet. It is at this time that the Antichrist has fully deceived the world and is given the power to persecute and destroy the people of God unimpeded for forty-two months (three-and-one-half years):

> "And the beast was given a mouth uttering haughty and blasphemous words, and it was allowed to exercise authority for forty-two months. It opened its mouth to utter blasphemies against God, blaspheming his name and his dwelling, that is, those who dwell in heaven. Also it was allowed to make war on the saints and to conquer them. And authority was given it over every tribe and people and language and nation, and all who dwell on earth will worship it, everyone whose name has not been written before the foundation of the world in the book of life of the Lamb who was slain. If anyone has an ear, let him hear: If anyone is to be taken captive, to captivity he goes; if anyone is to be slain with the sword, with the sword must he be slain. Here is a call for the endurance and faith of the saints" (Rev. 13:5-10).

> "He shall speak words against the Most High, and shall wear out the saints of the Most High, and shall think to change the times and the law; and they shall be given into his hand for a time, times, and half a time" (Dan. 7:25).

THE BEAST THROUGH THE TIME OF THE END

(Daniel 7:7–8,19; Revelation 13:1–18,17:6–18)

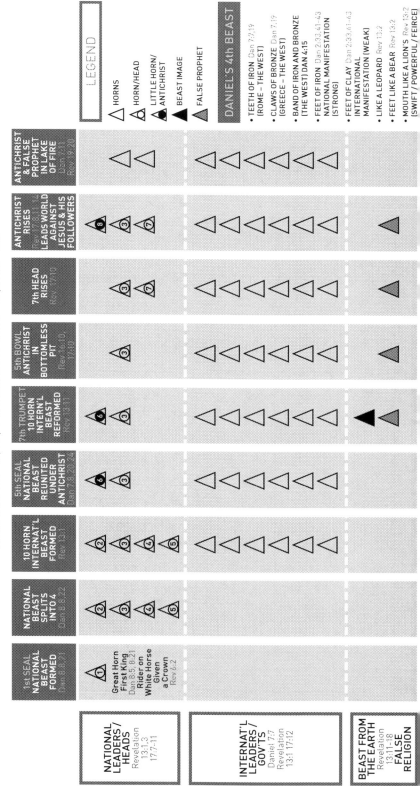

THE BEAST OF REVELATION (DANIEL'S FOURTH BEAST)

Terrifying and Dreadful and Exceedingly Strong...Stamped What Was Left with Its Feet (Daniel 7:7)

Timeline phases (top): JESUS RECEIVES SCROLL · SEALS BROKEN · SCROLL OPENED · FIRST SIDE OF SCROLL · SCROLL TURNED OVER · (time uncertain) · SECOND SIDE OF SCROLL

Events markers: Silence · Harvest of The Earth

Column headings: 1st–4th SEALS | 5th–6th SEALS | 7th SEAL | 1st–4th TRUMPET | 5th TRUMPET | 6th TRUMPET | 7th TRUMPET | 1st–4th BOWLS | 5th BOWL | 6th–7th BOWLS | Armies of Heaven With Jesus | 1000-Yr. Reign of Jesus | New Heaven New Earth

FALSE PROPHET (beast from the land)

- False Prophet Sets Up Abomination of Desolation
- False Prophet Leads Worship of Daniel's Little Horn
- World Religion Destroyed
- False Prophet Thrown Into Lake Of Fire

DANIEL'S LITTLE HORN (7:8 & 8:9) beast from the sea man of lawlessness (Human Manifestation of the beast)

- Restrainer Removed 2 Thess. 2:6-8
- Apostate Church Rebellion 2 Thess. 2:3
- 6th (8th) Head Directs National Leaders
- Lawlessness Reached Limit Dan. 8:23
- Man of Lawlessness Revealed 2 Thess. 2:4&8
- 6th (8th) Head Enters Into Covenant W/Israel
- 6th (8th) Head Breaks Covenant W/Israel
- 5th (8th) Head Leads As National Leader
- 8th Head Leads International Leaders
- 6th (8th) Head Loses National Base
- Lawless one Killed by the Breath of His Mouth 2 Thess. 2:8
- Beast Thrown Into Lake Of Fire

HEADS (national manifestation of the beast)

- 1st Head Falls Dan. 7:7
- 1st Head Splits 2nd, 3rd, 4th & 5th Heads Formed Dan. 7:7
- 2nd, 3rd, 4th & 5th Heads Rule
- 2nd, 4th, & 5th Heads Fall
- 6th Head Rules
- 6th & 8th Heads Are the Same
- 6th Head Falls
- 7th Head Replaces 6th; 3rd Head
- Beast That Was And Is Not
- Beast That Is to Come
- He Shall Be Broken Dan. 8:25

HORNS (international manifestation of the beast)

- 2nd, 3rd, 4th & 5th Heads Form Global Alliance Of 10 Horns Dan. 7:7
- 10 Horn-Global Alliance Rules
- 3 Horns (Heads) Removed by Little Horn Dan. 8:8
- Coming of the Lawless One 2 Thess. 2:9
- Takes His Seat in The Temple 2 Thess. 4
- 10-Horn Global Alliance Rules
- Beast Kingdom Plunged Into Darkness
- 10 Horns with Royal Authority

DEMONIC REALM

- Angel of Bottomless Pit Released
- THREE WOES
- 4 Angels of Euphrates Released
- Satan Thrown Down From Heaven
- Satan Possesses Little Horn
- Satan Bound
- Satan in Bottomless Pit
- Satan Loosed
- Satan Thrown Into Lake of Fire

As the leader of the Re-United States, the Antichrist leads the nation and the other nine governments as part of this 10-government alliance. We have already seen this alliance as the 10 toes of Nebuchadnezzar's image (Dan. 2:33, 41-43), the 10 horns of the fourth beast of Daniel 7 (Dan. 7:3-7), and here as the 10 horns of the beast of Revelation 13. But while the Antichrist is given authority for three-and-one-half years, at the fifth bowl, that power is taken away. Further discussion and description of the beast kingdom is found in the discussion of the scarlet beast in Revelation 17.

WORLD RELIGION
Beast out of the Earth - False Prophet

"Then I saw another beast rising out of the earth. It had two horns like a lamb and it spoke like a dragon. It exercises all the authority of the first beast in its presence, and makes the earth and its inhabitants worship the first beast, whose mortal wound was healed. It performs great signs, even making fire come down from heaven to earth in front of people, and by the signs that it is allowed to work in the presence of the beast it deceives those who dwell on earth, telling them to make an image for the beast that was wounded by the sword and yet lived. And it was allowed to give breath to the image of the beast, so that the image of the beast might even speak and might cause those who would not worship the image of the beast to be slain. Also it causes all, both small and great, both rich and poor, both free and slave, to be marked on the right hand or the forehead, so that no one can buy or sell unless he has the mark, that is, the name of the beast or the number of its name. This calls for wisdom: let the one who has understanding calculate the number of the beast, for it is the number of a man, and his number is 666" (Rev. 13:11-18).

In Revelation 13 we are introduced to a second beast called "the beast from out of the earth" (v. 11). This beast is incredibly important because although the Antichrist is filled with the power of Satan, he will not be working alone. He will have help in the form of this second beast, the false prophet. The false prophet acts in the authority of the first beast and can do signs and wonders to accomplish his will, giving further credibility to the beast in whose name he acts. Ultimately, the role of the false prophet is to drive not just obedience but worship of the beast. It is this worship, alongside the beast's declaration that he is God, that will reveal him to true believers.

Paul told us to watch for this key end-times sign two thousand years ago:

"Let no one deceive you in any way. For that day will not come, unless the rebellion comes first, and the man of lawlessness is revealed, the son of destruction, who opposes and exalts himself against every so-called god or object of worship, so that he takes his seat in the temple of God, proclaiming himself to be God" (2 Thess. 2:3-4).

"And then the lawless one will be revealed, whom the Lord Jesus will kill with the breath of his mouth and bring to nothing by the appearance of his coming. The coming of the lawless one is by the activity of Satan with all power and false signs and wonders, and with all wicked deception for those who are perishing, because they refused to love the truth and so be saved. Therefore God sends them a strong delusion, so that they may believe what is false, in order that all may be condemned who did not believe the truth but had pleasure in unrighteousness" (2 Thess. 2:8-12).

This revelation of the Antichrist through the support of the false prophet is also a sign of the end times mentioned by John. He, too, defines the Antichrist's emergence as the marker of the impending judgment of God.

"Children, it is the last hour, and as you have heard that antichrist is coming, so now many antichrists have come. Therefore we know that it is the last hour" (1 John 2:18).

WORLD ECONOMIC SYSTEM
Beast out of the Earth—The Image of The Beast

The first horn of the Beast out of the earth, the False Prophet, has those that dwell on earth make an image of the Beast and worship it. This image is then given breath that it might even speak (v.15) and make everyone receive a mark to participate in the world economic system (vv.16-17).

Although in the past the nature of this image has been difficult if not impossible to discern, today it has become increasingly obvious what this is referring to. With the development of artificial intelligence (AI) and other technologies, humans are now on the threshold of creating a god in their own image.

So, what does this god look like that was described almost two thousand years ago? From a technological perspective it will probably have multiple components all assembled to provide a form of omniscience that the AI, physically represented by the Image of the Beast, will share with the Antichrist. This Artificial Intelligence will be capable of processing an incomprehensible amount of information being fed to it through the internet and a network of satellites covering the entire planet. As the internet of things is further developed, everything will be providing information and surveillance that will assist enforcement of the Beast system. This information can be shared in real time with the Antichrist by way of a brain-computer interface, an electronic connection between the AI and the synapses of the Antichrist's brain.

But its omniscience is solidified with the advent of quantum computing. A quantum computing AI will have the ability to know all the encrypted communications transmitted electronically: commercial, private, diplomatic, financial, military, etc. throughout the world. It will have unlimited access to information and therefore ultimate control. If all electronic data is also being uploaded to the Antichrist through the beast system, he rises to the level of omnipotent (within a limited context relative to God).

Further evidence of the Antichrist's quantum capabilities can be found in Daniel 8:23. Although a minimalist description of this person, Daniel found it significant enough to state the following as it relates to the king of bold face, aka the Antichrist:

> "And at the latter end of their kingdom, when the transgressors have reached their limit, a king of bold face, *one who under-stands riddles*, shall arise" (Dan. 8:23, emphasis mine).

Other translations for *understanding riddles* include "understanding dark sentences," "skilled in intrigues," and "master of strategy."

These differing translations make clear the translators are struggling to provide a precise meaning. However, in the context of quantum computing, I believe the translation can be more precisely determined.

The Merriam Webster definition of riddle is "a mystifying, mislead-ing, or puzzling question posed as a problem to be solved or guessed: conundrum, *enigma*."

So, if you view encryption as a mathematical puzzle to be solved, this could very well be stating that the Antichrist will have this ability. Even in the definition of riddle the word enigma is used, which just so happens to be the name of the very first electro-mechanical rotor cipher machines used to encrypt German diplomatic and military communica-tions during WWII.

All this points to this beast system quite possibly consisting of the Antichrist with a neuro link to an AI quantum computer manifested in a robotic physical form as the Image of the Beast, aka the Abomination of Desolation, and of course, those that receive its mark. This is the ultimate idol, made by human hands (condemned throughout scripture), that becomes man's replacement of God as a super intelligent omniscient being. At the same time, it represents the ultimate inversion of truth with the arrogance of a man becoming god opposing Jesus who humbled himself as God and became a man.

With this technological Beast representing the culmination of Man's (and Satan's) ideal to dethrone God, it becomes even more apparent that the events described at the 5th Bowl are those of the Beast's destruction by God.

THE MARK OF THE BEAST

In a manner similar to God's sealing of his elect with the Holy Spirit, Satan uses a mark to identify his followers. This mark, which many believe will include the number 666, is initiated by the false prophet. In an effort to unify the world under Satan's control in rebellion against God, the mark is designed to identify the followers of Satan through their allegiance to the Antichrist. This allows believers, who will be identified by the fact that they will not have the mark, to be killed.

There is a great irony here. This shared hatred will create tremendous unity among unbelievers. However, unlike the unity among believers, this unity is unsustainable because it is built on a foundation of selfishness. In other words, the type of unity that the Antichrist is trying to gain ultimately won't work—and it cannot work—because inherent in the selfish base of that belief system is that it will break back down to the individual. In contrast, the unity provided in God through love is selfless, binding individuals together to such a degree that they cannot be separated. As Jesus promised, "I am in my Father, and you in me, and I in you" (John 14:20).

Seemingly, from the time John penned the words of this book, people have been trying to figure out the meaning of the identification 666. Speculation has become quite a distraction, even an industry. While it may not be fruitful to speculate on the actual name of the person who will fill the role of the Antichrist, it might be helpful to understand how his number will be used.

Scripture states that 666 is "the number of a man." The word "man" could be referring to an individual (somehow the number 666 is associated with the Antichrist himself) or it could be referring to mankind as a whole. It could also be referring to both. Biblically, the number seven is associated with divine perfection; six is associated with the attempt to attain perfection but missing the mark. Three sixes could also signify man (in this case, Antichrist) making himself God (three representing the trinity and six representing man who was created on the sixth day), which would be consistent with the view previously presented in the Beast Image comments.

Considering that the Antichrist will be able to track and persecute any he wishes, it is likely that 666 is symbolic and quite possibly associated with an individual's DNA sequence. Each one of us has a unique number (the number of a man) that no one else has. If you have someone's DNA sequence, you know as much as possible about them genetically. If you run those numbers through a system and apply global positioning technology, you can know who they are and where they are at all times. This would enable someone to create a unique identifier for each person with no chance of fraud. Coupled with an implanted RFID chip, GPS technology could easily become a reliable system of human identification, tracking, and transaction monitoring.

While this may seem intrusive and something that could never happen in this country, we must remember the chaos and destruction that will characterize this time. People will be desperate for peace and security. Thus the mark will provide the ultimate worldly solution to crime reduction and resource allocation. This will be desired during this period of worldwide instability.

"While people are saying, 'There is peace and security,' then sudden destruction will come upon them as labor pains come upon a pregnant woman, and they will not escape" (1 Thess. 5:3).

It is at this point in the theological interlude, immediately before John's description of God's full, unrestrained wrath, that the writer provides us with details on the rapture. We are about to read about this glorious event that occurred back at the seventh trumpet.

chapter eight
REDEMPTION
144,000 REDEEMED AS FIRSTFRUITS

*Then I looked, and behold, on Mount Zion stood the Lamb,
and with him 144,000 who had his name and his Father's
name written on their foreheads. And I heard a voice from
heaven like the roar of many waters and like the sound of
loud thunder. The voice I heard was like the sound of harpists
playing on their harps, and they were singing a new song before
the throne and before the four living creatures and before
the elders. No one could learn that song except the 144,000
who had been redeemed from the earth. It is these who have
not defiled themselves with women, for they are virgins. It is
these who follow the Lamb wherever he goes. These have been
redeemed from mankind as firstfruits for God and the Lamb,
and in their mouth no lie was found, for they are blameless.*

REVELATION 14:1-5

I n this passage, John revisits the 144,000 sealed believers who were
first introduced at the sixth seal. These redeemed from the nation
of Israel are taken alive directly from Mount Zion to the throne in
heaven. This occurs just prior to the catching up of all of the elect at
the rapture. These 144,000 are called "firstfruits," or the first reaping

of the larger harvest of believers. Jesus fulfilled the Feast of Firstfruits (1 Cor. 15:20) by presenting himself to the Father before appearing to his disciples after his resurrection (John 20:17, Luke 24:39; see also Appendix C). Likewise, these firstfruits present themselves around the throne of heaven.

The wording "firstfruits" draws on the agricultural symbolism so prevalent in ancient Israel. That this event ties in with the Feast of Firstfruits, in particular, is of great significance since it coincides with the transition of God's focus back to Israel.

Next we see God's final warning to those who dwell on the earth:

"Then I saw another angel flying directly overhead, with an eternal gospel to proclaim to those who dwell on earth, to every nation and tribe and language and people. And he said with a loud voice, 'Fear God and give him glory, because the hour of his judgment has come, and worship him who made heaven and earth, the sea and the springs of water.'

Another angel, a second, followed, saying, 'Fallen, fallen is Babylon the great, she who made all nations drink the wine of the passion of her sexual immorality.'

And another angel, a third, followed them, saying with a loud voice, 'If anyone worships the beast and its image and receives a mark on his forehead or on his hand, he also will drink the wine of God's wrath, poured full strength into the cup of his anger, and he will be tormented with fire and sulfur in the presence of the holy angels and in the presence of the Lamb. And the smoke of their torment goes up forever and ever, and they have no rest, day or night, these worshipers of the beast and its image, and whoever receives the mark of its name" (Rev. 14:6-11).

Following this vision, God forecasts the destruction of the world system and outlines the fate of those who choose to embrace it. What follows is unparalleled destruction, but just as God provides warning for those who rebel against his authority, he provides comfort to those who are about to lose their lives for his sake.

"I heard a voice from heaven saying, 'Write this: Blessed are the dead who die in the Lord from now on.' 'Blessed indeed,' says the Spirit, 'that they may rest from their labors, for their deeds follow them!'" (Rev. 14:13).

Although destruction follows, a special blessing is promised to those who heed God's warning and choose to follow him rather than the beast. This blessing is twofold: avoidance of God's unrestrained wrath on earth, followed by a future reward. This reward is revealed in Revelation 20:6—reigning with Jesus as priests for one thousand years. This dual warning and promise reminds us of the words of the Psalmist:

"Kiss the Son, lest he be angry, and you perish in the way, for his wrath is quickly kindled. Blessed are all who take refuge in him" (Psalm 2:12).

THE HARVEST OF THE EARTH
Feast of Trumpets

Tension is building in the narrative. Until now, those who came to faith in Jesus during the first five trumpets have been under intense persecution, Israel has been unrepentant, and God has restrained his wrath upon mankind. But the rapture is now on the horizon. As we will see, once the rapture occurs, no believers will remain on the earth. The persecution will cease, Israel will repent, and God's unrestrained wrath on mankind will begin.

It is at this point—Revelation 14:14-16—that John finally provides us with details on the harvest of the earth, which includes tantalizing details about the rapture of the church.

"Then I looked, and behold, a white cloud, and seated on the cloud one like a son of man, with a golden crown on his head, and a sharp sickle in his hand. And another angel came out of the temple, calling with a loud voice to him who sat on the cloud, 'Put in your sickle, and reap, for the hour to reap has come, for the harvest of the earth is fully ripe.' So he who sat on the cloud swung his sickle across the earth, and the earth was reaped" (Rev. 14:14-16).

The harvest is the ultimate fulfillment of two of Israel's fall feasts (see Appendix C) and has two phases. First is the harvest of believers, and as a result of the appearance of Christ in the sky to take his bride, the salvation of national Israel. The second phase is the rejection and destruction of the wicked.

The use of reaping imagery in this context is interesting. Each year, provided there was adequate rainfall, two harvests took place in Israel: the grain harvest and the grape harvest. Scripture frequently uses grain, a staple in Israel's diet, to symbolize life and God's bounty. Grapes, on the other hand, represent God's wrath. In the ancient presses, the grapes were crushed on the treading floor in preparation for being made into wine. After the grapes were ground and crushed (usually by human feet), their blood-red juice ran down through a small slit, where it was collected in a basin. This is the imagery here, and it is graphic. The winepress symbolizes the shedding of blood in battle. At the end of the trumpet judgments, God has come to the end of his patience with the wickedness of mankind and the earth is reaped. The wicked are about to be thrown into the crushing, bloody winepress of final judgment.

The grain harvest at the end of the seventh trumpet includes both the rapture of the church and the national salvation of Israel (Hosea 6:11, Isaiah 27:12-13). Most people are familiar with the rapture, but the salvation of Israel is often overlooked. Yet it is at this time that this supremely important end-times event occurs. This event was predicted in Hosea 5:15:

"I will return again to my place until they acknowledge their guilt and seek my face and in their distress earnestly seek me."

As the world witnesses Jesus gather the church (Rev. 1:7, Matt. 24:30), Israel's blindness is removed and she recognizes her Messiah (Zech. 12:10). At once, the people of Israel look, horrified, upon the Savior they once rejected. It is no wonder that the text is replete with imagery of tremendous mourning.

"And on that day…I will pour out on the house of David and the inhabitants of Jerusalem a spirit of grace and pleas for mercy, so that, when they look on me, on him whom they have pierced, they shall mourn for him, as one mourns for an only child, and weep bitterly over him, as one weeps over a firstborn" (Zech. 12:10-12; cf. Matt. 24:30; Rev. 1:7; Zech. 12:7-14; 13:1-9; Isaiah 30:19-21).

"At that time shall arise Michael, the great prince who has charge of your people. And there shall be a time of trouble, such as never has been since there was a nation till that time *[Israel's great tribulation]*. But at that time your people shall be delivered, everyone whose name shall be found written in the book" (Dan. 12:1, notation mine).

Israel's response of repentance is in stark contrast to her response to his first coming. At Jesus' first coming, those saying, "Blessed is the king who comes in the name of the Lord" (Luke 19:36-40) were met with rebuke by Israel's leaders. But now, Israel's recognition of her Messiah provokes the response of praise. Finally, the remnant of Israel will say, "Blessed is he who comes in the name of the Lord" (Matt 23:39).

Although the people of Israel finally repent, it will be too late for them to be taken up at the rapture. Instead, the sadness and horror they experience will lead them into a period of national mourning that coincides with the Days of Awe. The Days of Awe span ten days between the Feast of Trumpets and the Day of Atonement, which was Israel's highest holy day of the year. The Day of Atonement was the day on which the nation's corporate sin was fully atoned.

It is that corporate atonement we are seeing here. Israel recognizes her Messiah, and in her repentance, her sin is fully atoned. As a result, on the Day of Atonement, God restores Israel to blessing. We see this foretold in passages such as Hosea 6:11: "For you also, O Judah, a harvest is appointed, when I restore the fortunes of my people," as well as in Hosea 14:2-10 and Micah 7:18-20. We also see this prophesied in Deuteronomy, which speaks of the great blessing that comes once Israel has turned back to God:

"When you are in tribulation, and all these things come upon you in the latter days, you will return to the Lord your God and obey his voice. For the Lord your God is a merciful God. He will not leave you or destroy you or forget the covenant with your fathers that he swore to them" (Deut. 4:30-31).

"And when all these things come upon you, the blessing and the curse, which I have set before you, and you call them to mind among all the nations where the Lord your God has driven you, and return to the Lord your God, you and your children, and obey his voice in all that I command you today, with all your heart and with all your soul, then the Lord your God will restore your fortunes and have mercy on you, and he will gather you again from all the peoples where the Lord your God has scattered you… And he will make you more prosperous and numerous than your fathers. And the Lord your God will circumcise your heart and the heart of your offspring, so that you will love the Lord your God with all your heart and with all your soul, that you may live" (Deut. 30:1-6).

At this point, the rapture has occurred, the times of the Gentiles have been fulfilled (Luke 21:24), and with Israel having repented, she will be protected. This protection will remain throughout the bowl judgments (Jer. 32:37-38). This is a tremendous mercy on Israel because those judgments will be fierce. By this time, the earth will have experienced some of God's wrath in the trumpets, but now that the bowls are about to be poured out, mankind will experience God's full, unrestrained wrath.

TWO DIFFERENT EXPERIENCES OF THE HARVEST

Thus, while both the church and Israel are part of the same grain harvest, these two groups experience this harvest differently.

The church is resurrected and changed:

"Behold! I tell you a mystery. We shall not all sleep, but we shall all be changed, in a moment, in the twinkling of an eye, at the last trumpet. For the trumpet will sound, and the dead will be raised imperishable, and we shall be changed" (1 Cor. 15:51-52).

We also see this change described in the same agricultural symbolic language in 1 Corinthians 15:35-37:

"But someone will ask, 'How are the dead raised? With what kind of body do they come?' You foolish person! What you sow does not come to life unless it dies. And what you sow is not the body that is to be, but a bare kernel, perhaps of wheat or of some other *grain*" (emphasis mine).

Then the bride is taken up in the rapture and experiences cleansing on the sea of fire and glass (Rev. 15:2-4).

Meanwhile Israel, following her national repentance, must endure the cleansing of the threshing floor during the Days of Awe. This harvest is followed by the grape harvest in which the wicked are left to endure the winepress of God's bowl judgments (Rev. 14:17-20).

"Put in the sickle, for the harvest is ripe. Go in, tread, for the winepress is full. The vats overflow, for their evil is great" (Joel 3:13).

This order of events helps us understand 1 Corinthians 15:22-24, which outlines the order of God's redemptive plan: Jesus as firstfruits, then those who belong to him at his coming, and simultaneously the blessing of Israel through the national atonement of her people and her acceptance of Jesus as Messiah.

"For as in Adam all die, so also in Christ shall all be made alive. But each in his own order: Christ the firstfruits, then at his coming those who belong to Christ. Then comes the end, when he delivers the kingdom to God the Father after destroying every rule and every authority and power" (1 Cor. 15:22-24).

When Jesus comes for his redeemed and Israel receives her blessing, we have reached the beginning of the end.

CONFIRMING THE ORDER

One of the wonderful things about Scripture is how patterns and events are confirmed elsewhere. That is the case here. We find all of these events related to the harvest of the earth - the resurrection of the dead, the national salvation of Israel, and her protection as the wrath of God is poured out upon the unbelieving world - described in Isaiah 26:19-21 hundreds of years earlier:

> "Your dead shall live; their bodies shall rise.
>   You who dwell in the dust, awake and sing for joy!
> For your dew is a dew of light,
>   and the earth will give birth to the dead.
> Come, my people, enter your chambers,
>   and shut your doors behind you;
> hide yourselves for a little while
>   until the fury has passed by.
> For behold, the Lord is coming out from his place
>   to punish the inhabitants of the earth for their iniquity,
> and the earth will disclose the blood shed on it,
>   and will no more cover its slain."

Once again, we have all of the key events in the same order we have seen in Revelation. Isaiah first describes the resurrection of the dead. Then Israel is called into her chambers for protection while God punishes the inhabitants of the earth. It is at this time, when the bridegroom leaves his chambers (Joel 2:16-18), that Israel calls a great assembly, recognizing that she has missed the wedding:

> "Gather the people. Consecrate the congregation;
>   assemble the elders; gather the children,
> even nursing infants. Let the bridegroom leave his room,
>   and the bride her chamber.

Between the vestibule and the altar
  let the priests, the ministers of the Lord, weep
and say, 'Spare your people, O Lord,
  and make not your heritage a reproach,
a byword among the nations. Why should they say among the peoples,
  'Where is their God?'
Then the Lord became jealous for his land
  and had pity on his people."

We also see this reference to a wedding in the parable of the ten virgins as Jesus' end-times discourse continues into Matthew 25. At the harvest of the earth, the bride, represented in the parable as the five wise virgins with oil, has been taken up in preparation for the marriage supper of the Lamb. But Israel, the five foolish virgins without oil, is prevented from entering. Through the tribulation of this period, however, Israel's heart is changed and she now seeks her true Messiah but has not yet come to know him. It is at this moment, as she looks upon Jesus, that her blindness is removed and she is stirred to repentance.

"Then the kingdom of heaven will be like ten virgins who took their lamps and went to meet the bridegroom. Five of them were foolish, and five were wise. For when the foolish took their lamps, they took no oil with them, but the wise took flasks of oil with their lamps. As the bridegroom was delayed, they all became drowsy and slept. But at midnight there was a cry, 'Here is the bridegroom! Come out to meet him.' Then all those virgins rose and trimmed their lamps. And the foolish said to the wise, 'Give us some of your oil, for our lamps are going out.' But the wise answered, saying, 'Since there will not be enough for us and for you, go rather to the dealers and buy for yourselves.' And while they were going to buy, the bridegroom came, and those who were ready went in with him to the marriage feast, and the door was shut. Afterward the other virgins came also, saying, 'Lord, lord, open to us.' But he answered, 'Truly, I say to you, I do not know you.' Watch therefore, for you know neither the day nor the hour" (Matt. 25:1-13).

A CLOSER LOOK AT THE RAPTURE

The timing of the rapture is a subject of great confusion, so let's take a closer look at this glorious event. How can we be so sure that it occurs at the seventh trumpet? Are there additional Scriptures that confirm this timing?

The first confirmation comes in the overlay of Revelation 14:14–16, which we have identified as the rapture, and 1 Corinthians 15:52 and 1 Thessalonians 4:16, which provide key details of the event. All three verses are associated with a very particular aspect of the rapture—the blowing of the final trumpet of God. 1 Corinthians 15:52 uses the phrase "at the last trump." 1 Thessalonians 4:16 uses the phrase "with the trump of God." The only trumpets mentioned in the book of Revelation are those blown by the angels. A simple reading of the text would suggest, therefore, that the last trump is the seventh trumpet. It just so happens that the harvest of the earth is, in fact, described at the seventh trumpet in language that mirrors that of 1 Thessalonians 4:16-17.

> "Then I looked, and behold, a white cloud, and seated on the cloud one like a son of man, with a golden crown on his head, and a sharp sickle in his hand. And another angel came out of the temple, calling with a loud voice to him who sat on the cloud, 'Put in your sickle, and reap, for the hour to reap has come, for the harvest of the earth is fully ripe.' So he who sat on the cloud swung his sickle across the earth, and the earth was reaped" (Rev. 14:14-16).

> "For the Lord himself will descend from heaven with a cry of command, with the voice of an Archangel, and with the sound of the trumpet of God. And the dead in Christ will rise first. Then we who are alive, who are left, will be caught up together

with them in the clouds to meet the Lord in the air, and so we will always be with the Lord" (1 Thess. 4:16-17).

"Behold! I tell you a mystery. We shall not all sleep, but we shall be changed, in a moment, in the twinkling of an eye, at the last trumpet. For the trumpet will sound, and the dead will be raised imperishable, and we shall be changed" (1 Cor. 15:51-52).

It is at this point in Revelation—at the seventh trumpet, immediately before God's unrestrained wrath—that the rapture occurs.

As we can see from these and other verses (including Revelation 1:7), the rapture is not a secret event. It is witnessed by everyone living on earth. It begins in the east and moves to the west (Luke 17:24, Matt. 24:27). It will be observed, in person, by every individual without the aid of human technology (Matt. 24:30).

Jesus, too, described this time in the Gospels. Note that in these passages, we see his second coming and the harvest described in the same sequence as in the book of Revelation:

"Then will appear in heaven, the sign of the Son of Man, and then all the tribes of the earth will mourn, and they will see the Son of Man coming on the clouds of heaven with power and great glory. And he will send out his Angels with a loud trumpet call, and they will gather His elect from the four winds, from one end of heaven to the other" (Matt. 24:30-31).

"And then they will see the Son of Man coming in clouds with great power and glory. And then he will send out the angels and gather his elect from the four winds, from the ends of the earth to the ends of heaven" (Mark 13:26-27).

"And then they will see the Son of Man coming in a cloud with power and great glory. Now when these things begin to take place, straighten up and raise your heads, because your redemption is drawing near" (Luke 21:27-28).

Although the wording in all three passages may be slightly different, each passage is clearly describing different aspects of the same event.

It is also worth noting that this event cannot occur at Christ's second coming since there will be no elect remaining on earth at that time, with the exception of Israel, who is not gathered until the final judgement. (cf. Rev. 13:16-17; Rev. 16:9,11)

A second confirmation is the relationship between the rapture and the mystery of God.

> "[B]ut that in the days of the *trumpet call* to be sounded by the seventh angel, the *mystery of God* would be fulfilled" (Rev. 10:7, emphasis mine).

What is the mystery of God? At this point we may not know, but we are told that at the seventh trumpet, the mystery will be fulfilled (Rev. 10:7). Now look at 1 Corinthians 15:51, which tells us a portion of what this mystery is.

> *"Behold! I tell you a mystery.* We shall not all sleep, but we shall be changed, in a moment, in the twinkling of an eye, at the last trumpet. For the trumpet will sound, and the dead will be raised imperishable, and we shall be changed" (1 Cor. 15:51-52, emphasis mine).

The "mystery" is the rapture!

We see another tie-in between the seventh trumpet rapture and this "mystery" in Romans 11. In a chronological view of Revelation, the national redemption of Israel occurs immediately after the rapture of the church. In Romans 11, Paul not only ties the rapture to the mystery, but he ties in the national redemption of Israel, as well:

> "Lest you be wise in your own sight, I want you to *understand this mystery,* brothers: a partial hardening has come upon Israel, until the fullness of the Gentiles has come in. And in this way all Israel will be saved, as it is written, 'The Deliverer will come from Zion, he will banish ungodliness from Jacob; and this will be my covenant with them when I take away their sins'" (Rom. 11:25-27, emphasis mine).

Taken together, these verses tie the rapture and the national redemption of Israel through the mystery of God at the seventh trumpet.

MARTYRDOM BEFORE WRATH / RAPTURE BEFORE WRATH / PROTECTION THROUGH WRATH—ALWAYS

There is one last detail to tie together. A common belief is that the rapture must occur prior to the opening of the seals because we are not destined for wrath (1 Thess. 1:10, 5:9, Romans 5:9), but does this really support a pre-seal rapture? Regardless of where you place God's wrath in the chronology of Revelation, God's wrath doesn't occur until after the first six seals are completed. Consider the following:

Seal judgments—man's wrath:

The seals are man's wrath against man, not God's wrath against man. They are the result of events like war (or the consequences of war), competition for goods, and the persecution of the saints. If God's wrath isn't poured out in the seal judgments, then the rapture doesn't need to precede them either.

Trumpet judgments—God's restrained wrath:

The trumpet judgments are part of God's wrath upon the earth, but his wrath is selective and restrained during this time. The church will be martyred prior to the trumpets, so the church will not experience God's wrath. People who repent and believe during the trumpets will receive the seal of God on their foreheads, which protects them from his wrath (Rev. 9:4). Ultimately, these post-seal believers will be protected from God's wrath either by removal from the earth by martyrdom at the hands of the false prophet or through God's hand of protection until their removal at the harvest of the earth (the rapture).

Bowl judgments—God's wrath in full force:

The full force of God's wrath will only be felt during the bowl judgments, which will be cut short (Matt. 24:22). Repentant

Israel will be protected during this time. Those who repent during the first three bowls will be martyred.

All of these facts argue against a pretribulation (pre-seal) rapture. The key point is that upon believing, God's wrath is no longer directed toward that individual. Man's wrath is, but not God's.

THE 1,335 DAYS
Yom Kippur—Israel's Day of Atonement

"The earth has yielded its increase;
God, our God, shall bless us.
God shall bless us;
let all the ends of the earth fear him!" (Psalm 67:6-7).

We have discussed two very important events that occur during the harvest of the earth, but there is one more element that we have yet to discuss. That is the end of the 1,335 days.

At the harvest of the earth, three events are actually coming together:

- The rapture

- The salvation of national Israel

- The end of the 1,335 days of Daniel 12.

We have discussed the rapture and the harvest of the earth, but what of the 1,335 days? This period of time comes from Daniel 12:12: "Blessed is he who waits and arrives at the 1,335 days." This period will occur between the time the burnt offering is taken away and will conclude with a blessing for those (of Israel) who make it to the end of this time. By putting together the pieces of prophecy, we see that this blessing refers to the restoration of Israel, which occurs at Yom Kippur following the ten Days of Awe beginning at the harvest of the earth (the rapture). Therefore, if the national salvation of Israel occurs at the seventh trumpet, then the 1,335 days end here, too.

The first place we see discussion of this blessing is in Isaiah 27, where it is associated with the blowing of the trumpet that occurs at the grain harvest.

"In that day from the river Euphrates to the Brook of Egypt the Lord will thresh out the *grain*, and you will be gleaned one by one, O people of Israel. And in that day *a great trumpet will be blown*, and those who were lost in the land of Assyria and those who were driven out to the land of Egypt will come and worship the Lord on the holy mountain at Jerusalem" (Isa. 27:12-13, emphasis mine).

Here we see the same combination of elements we've seen before: the blowing of the trumpet, the grain harvest, and the national restoration of Israel. Once Israel recognizes her mistake in rejecting Jesus and embraces him as Messiah, the atonement of Israel will be complete and the people's sin will be remembered no more. Verses such as Jeremiah 31:31-40 (also see Jeremiah 33:14-26 and Zechariah 3:8-10; 12:7-14; 13:1-9) describe this as the Lord making a new covenant with his people:

"For the children of Israel shall abide many days without king or prince, without sacrifice or sacred pillar, without ephod or teraphim. Afterward the children of Israel shall return and seek the Lord their God and David their king. They shall fear the Lord and his goodness in the latter days" (Hos. 3:4-5).

"Thus says the Lord:
'As the new wine is found in the cluster,
     and they say, "Do not destroy it,
     for there is a *blessing* in it,"
     so I will do for my servants' sake,
     and not destroy them all.
I will bring forth offspring from Jacob,
     and from Judah possessors of my mountains;
     my chosen shall possess it,
     and my servants shall dwell there.
Sharon shall become a pasture for flocks,
     and the Valley of Achor a place for herds to lie down,

for my people who have sought me'"
(Isa. 65:8-10 emphasis mine).

"On that day there shall be a fountain opened for the house of David and the inhabitants of Jerusalem, to cleanse them from sin and uncleanness. And on that day, declares the Lord of hosts, I will cut off the names of the idols from the land, so that they shall be remembered no more. And also I will remove from the land the prophets and the spirit of uncleanness. . . . They will call upon my name, and I will answer them. I will say, 'They are my people'; and they will say, 'The Lord is my God'" (Zech. 13:1-9).

"I will sprinkle clean water on you, and you shall be clean from all your uncleannesses, and from all your idols I will cleanse you. And I will give you a new heart, and a new spirit I will put within you. And I will remove the heart of stone from your flesh and give you a heart of flesh. And I will put my Spirit within you, and cause you to walk in my statutes and be careful to obey my rules" (Eze. 36:25-27; also see Eze. 37:23; Joel 2:17-32).

This occurs at the grain harvest. While the national repentance occurs too late for Israel to be taken in the rapture, her people receive the blessing of national atonement. Israel will have to endure the persecution of the Antichrist, but she will be protected through the bowl judgments. It will be clear that Israel is under God's protection, and all those who once scoffed at her misfortunes and mocked her, saying, "Where is your God?" will be put to shame. Israel will no longer be a "reproach among the nations" (Joel 2:17-32; Zephaniah 3). Instead, she will rejoice in a new relationship with God—one based on trust and faith:

"Come, let us return to the Lord; for he has torn us, that he may heal us; he has struck us down, and he will bind us up. After two days he will revive us; on the third day he will raise us up, that we may live before him. Let us know; let us press on to know the Lord; his going out is sure as the dawn; he will come to us as the showers, as the spring rains that water the earth" (Hos. 6:1-3).

"It will be said on that day, 'Behold, this is our God; we have waited for him, that he might save us. This is the Lord; we have waited for him; let us be glad and rejoice in his salvation'" (Isa. 25:9).

What a change from the first century when Israel abandoned Jesus and handed him over to be crucified! Just after his prophecy regarding the end times in the Olivet Discourse, Jesus mourned, "O Jerusalem, Jerusalem, the city that kills the prophets and stones those who are sent to it! How often would I have gathered your children together as a hen gathers her brood under her wings, and you would not! See, your house is left to you desolate. For I tell you, you will not see me again, until you say, 'Blessed is he who comes in the name of the Lord'" (Matt. 23:37-39). At that time, even the high priest abandoned him (Matt. 26:63-65).

Even though Israel rejected Jesus in the first century, God had a plan. We see that plan unveiled in Revelation. Even the apostle Paul was expecting national repentance of Israel during the end times.

"Lest you be wise in your own sight, I want you to understand this mystery, brothers: a partial hardening has come upon Israel, until the fullness of the Gentiles has come in. And in this way all Israel will be saved, as it is written, The Deliverer will come from Zion, he will banish ungodliness from Jacob; and this will be my covenant with them when I take away their sins" (Rom. 11:25-27).

There was once a "partial hardening," but that hardening extends only to the rapture. Then Israel will be saved.

Further down in the verse, Paul writes of Israel: "As regards election they are beloved for the sake of their forefathers and the calling of God is irrevocable" (v. 29). This tells us clearly that, although it may seem as if God is far away from Israel right now, the Redeemer is not finished with her. What a picture of God's faithfulness! God is not finished with Israel and will fulfill all his promises given through his prophets. However, this should not suggest in any way that the rapture must occur prior to the beginning of Daniel's Seventieth Week—Israel's tribulation.

A PICTURE OF GOD'S FAITHFULNESS

Let's look again at all that has transpired to this point. Prior to the tribulation, Israel's call to repentance goes unheeded (Rev. 10:1-11). As a result, Israel accepts the Antichrist (Daniel's little horn), who leads the nation into tribulation during Daniel's Seventieth Week (Rev. 11:1-14). During the first three-and-one-half years of this seven-year period, the two witnesses (Elijah and perhaps Enoch) prepare the hearts of Israel to accept Jesus (Mal. 4:5).

During this time, one-third of Israel is killed by the mounted troops released by the four angles at the Euphrates River. Of the remaining two-thirds, half are killed in Jerusalem and half flee into exile, fulfilling Zechariah 13:8. Yet at the appearance of Jesus in the clouds, the blindness of Israel is lifted (Zech. 13:9). Upon seeing him, Israel repents and accepts her Savior, and the remnant of Israel is saved. Now that Israel is his, Jesus protects them and begins the restorative process as promised throughout prophecy.

This fulfills the promise of Daniel 9:24 for the Seventieth Week: "to finish the transgression, to put an end to sin, and to atone for iniquity, to bring in everlasting righteousness, to seal both vision and prophet." This occurs on the highest holy day of the Jewish calendar, Yom Kippur, the Day of Atonement. Israel is about to enter into everlasting righteousness. It is no wonder Daniel wrote: "Blessed is he who waits and arrives at the 1,335 days" (Dan. 12:12)!

GRAPE HARVEST
WINEPRESS OF GOD COMMENCES
(Culminates Revelation 19:15)

"Then another angel came out of the temple in heaven, and he too had a sharp sickle. And another angel came out from the altar, the angel who has authority over the fire, and he called with a loud voice to the one who had the sharp sickle, 'Put in your sickle and gather the clusters from the vine of the earth, for its grapes are ripe.' So the angel swung his sickle across the earth and gathered the grape harvest of the earth and threw it into the great winepress of the wrath of God. And the winepress was trodden outside the city, and blood flowed from the winepress, as high as a horse's bridle, for 1,600 stadia" (Rev. 14:17-20).

"From his mouth comes a sharp sword with which to strike down the nations, and he will rule them with a rod of iron. He will tread the winepress of the fury of the wrath of God the Almighty" (Rev. 19:15).

The grape harvest extends from the harvest of the earth to the return of Jesus with the armies of heaven (Rev. 19:14). This period is also described as the winepress of God (Rev. 19:15). During this time, the seven bowls of God's wrath are poured out on the unrepentant world. God's patience is finally at an end, and his wrath is about to be unleashed without restraint. Had this time not been cut short, Jesus said, "no human would be saved" (Matt. 24:22). The blood flowing from the winepress (Rev. 14:20) looks forward to the culmination of God's wrath (Rev. 19:15).

The imagery of God's fury as being like a winepress is a familiar image in Scripture. Certainly the first-century audience would have associated it with the imagery from Isaiah 63:

"Who is this who comes from Edom, in crimsoned garments from Bozrah, he who is splendid in his apparel, marching in the greatness of his strength? 'It is I, speaking in righteousness, mighty to save.' Why is your apparel red, and your garments like his who treads in the winepress? 'I have trodden the winepress alone, and from the peoples no one was with me; I trod them in my anger and trampled them in my wrath; their lifeblood spattered on my garments, and stained all my apparel. For the day of vengeance was in my heart, and my year of redemption had come. I looked, but there was no one to help; I was appalled, but there was no one to uphold; so my own arm brought me salvation, and my wrath upheld me. I trampled down the peoples in my anger; I made them drunk in my wrath, and I poured out their lifeblood on the earth'" (Isa. 63:1-6).

Other prophets, such as Zechariah and Zephaniah, also talk about this terrifying judgment. Now at the appointed time, God will manifest his power, save his people, and use them as a testimony of his greatness to an unbelieving world (see especially Zechariah 12:2-6).

SEA OF GLASS AND FIRE
Purification of the non-Martyred Elect

"Then I saw another sign in heaven, great and amazing, seven angels with seven plagues, which are the last, for with them the wrath of God is finished.

And I saw what appeared to be a sea of glass mingled with fire—and also those who had conquered the beast and its image and the number of its name, standing beside the sea of glass with harps of God in their hands. And they sing the song of Moses, the servant of God, and the song of the Lamb, saying,

'Great and amazing are your deeds,
O Lord God the Almighty!
Just and true are your ways,
O King of the nations!
Who will not fear, O Lord,
and glorify your name?
For you alone are holy.
All nations will come
and worship you,
for your righteous acts have been revealed.'

After this I looked, and the sanctuary of the tent of witness in heaven was opened, and out of the sanctuary came the seven angels with the seven plagues, clothed in pure, bright linen, with golden sashes around their chests" (Rev. 15:1-6).

Earlier, just after the institution of the mark of the beast by the false prophet, a special blessing is given to those who refuse the mark (Rev. 14:13). We see that promise being fulfilled here. However, this promise is fulfilled differently for different groups of people. Those who overcome the beast prior to the harvest of the earth are seen by the sea of glass and fire. Those refusing the mark following the harvest of the earth are promised participation in the first resurrection (Rev. 20:4-6). Together this group of elect reigns as priests with Jesus for one thousand years.

Those escaping the winepress of God enjoy the presence of God on the sea of glass seen around his throne. We have seen this sea of glass before (Rev. 4:6), but this time, there is fire. The addition of fire in the form of torches or lamps before the throne of God suggests the purification process by the Holy Spirit preparing these individuals for such an encounter.

This is a fulfillment of the promise in 1 Corinthians 3:11-15 and Luke 3:17:

> "For no one can lay a foundation other than that which is laid, which is Jesus Christ. Now if anyone builds on the foundation with gold, silver, precious stones, wood, hay, straw—each one's work will become manifest, for the Day will disclose it, because it will be revealed by fire, and the fire will test what sort of work each one has done. If the work that anyone has built on the foundation survives, he will receive a reward. If anyone's work is burned up, he will suffer loss, though he himself will be saved, but only as through fire" (1 Cor. 3:11-15).

> "His winnowing fork is in his hand, to clear his threshing floor and to gather the wheat into his barn, but the chaff he will burn with unquenchable fire" (Luke 3:17).

We also saw the promise of this coming purification when John the Baptist compared his baptism to Jesus' saying, "I baptize you with water, but he who is mightier than I is coming, the strap of whose sandals I am not worthy to untie. He will baptize you with the Holy Spirit and with fire" (Luke 3:16).

Those not escaping the winepress of God encounter fire of another sort, the lake of fire:

> "Then Death and Hades were thrown into the lake of fire. This is the second death, the lake of fire. And if anyone's name was not found written in the book of life, he was thrown into the lake of fire" (Rev. 20:14-15).

> "Do not be deceived: God is not mocked, for whatever one sows, that will he also reap" (Gal. 6:7).

The unrighteous will receive full and just judgment for their works.

In Jesus' end-times discourse in Matthew 24–25, we learn from the parable of the ten talents what it will be like for the elect on the sea of glass and fire, which is the judgment seat of Christ:

> "For it will be like a man going on a journey, who called his servants and entrusted to them his property. To one he gave five talents, to another two, to another one, to each according to his ability. Then he went away. He who had received the five talents went at once and traded with them, and he made five talents more. So also he who had the two talents made two talents more. But he who had received the one talent went and dug in the ground and hid his master's money. Now after a long time the master of those servants came and settled accounts with them. And he who had received the five talents came forward, bringing five talents more, saying, 'Master, you delivered to me five talents; here I have made five talents more.' His master said to him, 'Well done, good and faithful servant. You have been faithful over a little; I will set you over much. Enter into the joy of your master.' And he also who had the two talents came forward, saying, 'Master, you delivered to me two talents; here I have made two talents more.' His master said to him, 'Well done, good and faithful servant. You have been faithful over

a little; I will set you over much. Enter into the joy of your master.' He also who had received the one talent came forward, saying, 'Master, I knew you to be a hard man, reaping where you did not sow, and gathering where you scattered no seed, so I was afraid, and I went and hid your talent in the ground. Here you have what is yours.' But his master answered him, 'You wicked and slothful servant! You knew that I reap where I have not sown and gather where I scattered no seed? Then you ought to have invested my money with the bankers, and at my coming I should have received what was my own with interest. So take the talent from him and give it to him who has the ten talents. For to everyone who has will more be given, and he will have an abundance. But from the one who has not, even what he has will be taken away. And cast the worthless servant into the outer darkness. In that place there will be weeping and gnashing of teeth'" (Matt. 25:14-30).

But before the people of the earth stand before the final judgment seat, they must first endure the bowls of God's wrath. This is what we are about to see.

chapter nine

SEVEN BOWLS GOD'S UNRESTRAINED WRATH

THE BOWL JUDGMENTS BEGIN

And one of the four living creatures gave to the seven angels seven golden bowls full of the wrath of God who lives forever and ever, and the sanctuary was filled with smoke from the glory of God and from his power, and no one could enter the sanctuary until the seven plagues of the seven angels were finished.

REVELATION 15:7-8

The time for waiting is over. It is time for the seven bowls of the wrath of God to be poured out upon the earth.

First Bowl
PAINFUL SORES ON MARK BEARERS

"Then I heard a loud voice from the temple telling the seven angels, "Go and pour out on the earth the seven bowls of the wrath of God." So the first angel went and poured out his bowl on the earth, and harmful and painful sores came upon the people who bore the mark of the beast and worshiped its image" (Rev. 16:1-2).

Here we see the beginning of judgment on those worshipping the beast. We know from the story of Job how painful these sores can be. Job scraped his sores with shards of pottery just to find a small amount of relief. However, there will be those who have not yet received the mark who will not receive this judgment. Even at this time, there will still be those who refuse the mark, repent, and are saved.

Second Bowl
ALL IN THE SEA DIE

"The second angel poured out his bowl into the sea, and it became like the blood of a corpse, and every living thing died that was in the sea" (Rev. 16:3).

At this point, all of the world's sea plants and sea creatures die. This will put real pressure on the world's food supply. Even now, there are still those who repent and are saved (inferred from Revelation 16:9 and 16:11).

Third Bowl
FRESH WATER BECOMES BLOOD

"The third angel poured out his bowl into the rivers and the springs of water, and they became blood. And I heard the angel in charge of the waters say, 'Just are you, O Holy One, who is and who was, for you brought these judgments. For they have shed the blood of saints and prophets, and you have given them blood to drink. It is what they deserve!' And I heard the altar saying, 'Yes, Lord God the Almighty, true and just are your judgments!'" (Rev. 16:4-7).

This is the last period during which there will be those who do not take the mark, repent, and are saved (inferred from Revelation 16:9 and 16:11).

Satan, through the beast and the false prophet, has continued to be successful in killing all the followers of Jesus except those numbered among the people of Israel. At this point, he turns his attention back to Israel to destroy God's final witness on the earth. Even so, God's plan is not thwarted. As we will see, God will use Satan's attempt to destroy Israel as his final witness to the nations.

"And my holy name I will make known in the midst of my people Israel, and I will not let my holy name be profaned any more. And the nations shall know that I am the Lord, the Holy One in Israel" (Eze. 39:7).

Fourth Bowl
SUN SCORCHES MAN

"The fourth angel poured out his bowl on the sun, and it was allowed to scorch people with fire. They were scorched by the fierce heat, and they cursed the name of God who had power over these plagues. They did not repent and give him glory" (Rev. 16:8-9).

At this time, people are tormented with extreme heat. Think of the hottest day you can imagine or the heat of Death Valley blazing down on you. Now imagine that there is no relief. All of those still alive, excluding Israel, have the mark of the beast. From this point on, there is no more repentance.

Fifth Bowl
BEAST'S THRONE AND KINGDOM PLUNGED INTO DARKNESS
The 2,300 Days
(Sixth Head Falls)

"The fifth angel poured out his bowl on the throne of the beast, and its kingdom was plunged into darkness. People gnawed their tongues in anguish and cursed the God of heaven for their pain and sores. They did not repent of their deeds" (Rev. 16:10-11).

During the fifth bowl, the beast's kingdom is plunged into darkness. Since no restriction of natural light sources is mentioned during the bowls (as it is in the trumpets), this is not likely referring to natural darkness. So what is it referring to? There are two options.

The first option is that it is referring to the destruction of the technological infrastructure underpinning the beast nation, thus the earth "going dark" in a technological sense. This could be caused by a natural event - a coronal mass ejection on the sun - or a manmade event such as an upper atmosphere nuclear detonation that produces an electromagnetic pulse destroying the electronics and power source(s) necessary to run the systems. The beast's heavily technologically de-pendent system (government, military, economy) collapses, but only after it has accomplished the task of clearly distinguishing the followers of the beast from the followers of God. Without the technological infrastructure, the beast nation loses its international dominance.

The second option is that this darkness could be referring to a literal place into which the beast is plunged. We know from Revelation 11:7, 17:8 that the beast rises from the bottomless pit, a place of darkness if correctly equated with Jude 1:6 and Revelation 9:2. Whether it refers to a destruction of the beast nation's technological infrastructure or whether it refers to the darkness of the pit or both, this sudden darkness ends the reign of the sixth head (the Antichrist), which occurs 2,300 days following the taking away of the burnt offering as predicted in Daniel 8:13-14:

> "For how long is the vision concerning the regular burnt offer-
> ing, the transgression that makes desolate, and the giving over of
> the sanctuary and host to be trampled under foot? And he said
> to me, 'For 2300 evenings and mornings. Then the sanctuary
> shall be restored to its rightful state'" (Dan. 8:13-14).

At the end of the 2,300 days, the occupation of Israel is complete and the Antichrist (leading the Re-United States) must withdraw his forces, leaving Israel without protection from other hostile nations. The Antichrist's occupation extends from the sixth trumpet until his loss of power here at the fifth bowl. By this time, he will have destroyed

Israel's immediate neighbors, Egypt and Syria (Dan. 11:40-43) and Israel will have no immediate regional threat. Even so, the retreat of the Antichrist creates the appearance of vulnerability to other hostile forces. Fortunately, Scripture tells us that Israel dwells securely under Jesus' divine protection.

It is immediately after this time that a seventh national leader of the beast nation, the Re-United States, takes control of the seat of power vacated by the Antichrist. There is no more information given to us about this head. We only know from Revelation 17:10 that the one who "is" can be identified as the third head and the "one who is to come" is the seventh.

Sixth Bowl
THE WHOLE WORLD PREPARED FOR BATTLE AT ARMAGEDDON

"The sixth angel poured out his bowl on the great river Euphrates, and its water was dried up, to prepare the way for the kings from the east. And I saw, coming out of the mouth of the dragon and out of the mouth of the beast and out of the mouth of the false prophet, three unclean spirits like frogs. For they are demonic spirits, performing signs, who go abroad to the kings of the whole world, to assemble them for battle on the great day of God the Almighty" (Rev. 16:12-14).

With the destruction of the beast nation's infrastructure, the Antichrist loses his power to dominate the international alliance. He still exists, but he abandons the Re-United States as it no longer offers him a power base from which to work.

Seeking an alternative means of consolidating power over the international alliance, the Antichrist turns to spiritual deception of the world leaders (the ten horns). This is accomplished by three unclean spirits emanating from the mouths of Satan, the Antichrist, and the false prophet. These spirits move like frogs between the world leaders and have one goal: to prepare mankind for battle with God. These world leaders succumb to this deception and act according to the will of Satan without understanding the truth and the real nature of the battle.

To accomplish his ultimate purposes, we see God drying up the great river Euphrates, perhaps a result of the extreme heat encountered during the fourth bowl. This allows the "kings of the whole world" to assemble. But while these leaders think they are arraying against Israel (Ezekiel 38), they are actually being called to battle against God himself. Ironically, while mankind thinks the Euphrates drying up is a benefit in their plans against Israel, it actually serves as an invitation to participate in their own destruction. The nearness of Christ's coming is emphasized by the call to stay awake.

> "Behold, I am coming like a thief! Blessed is the one who stays awake, keeping his garments on, that he may not go about naked and be seen exposed!" (Rev. 16:15).

Seventh Bowl
ARMAGEDDON

> "And they assembled them at the place that in Hebrew is called Armageddon. The seventh angel poured out his bowl into the air, and a loud voice came out of the temple, from the throne, saying, 'It is done!' And there were flashes of lightning, rumblings, peals of thunder, and a great earthquake such as there had never been since man was on the earth, so great was that earthquake. The great city was split into three parts, and the cities of the nations fell, and God remembered Babylon the great, to make her drain the cup of the wine of the fury of his wrath. And every island fled away, and no mountains were to be found. And great hailstones, about one hundred pounds each, fell from heaven on people; and they cursed God for the plague of the hail, because the plague was so severe" (Rev. 16:16-21).

It may read as foolishness to us now, but the people of the world will gather at the plain of Armageddon to fight against God himself. This is the power of spiritual deception. The kings of the earth gather, but only in preparation for their own destruction because it is prophesied that Jesus—and Jesus alone—will ultimately sit on the throne of Zion.

"Why do the nations rage
　　and the peoples plot in vain?
The kings of the earth set themselves,
　　and the rulers take counsel together,
　　against the Lord and against his Anointed, saying,
'Let us burst their bonds apart
　　and cast away their cords from us.'
He who sits in the heavens laughs;
　　the Lord holds them in derision.
Then he will speak to them in his wrath,
　　and terrify them in his fury, saying,
　　'As for me, I have set my King
　　on Zion, my holy hill'" (Psalm 2:1-6).

Zephaniah also describes this deception as part of God's plan to gather the nations for destruction:

"'Therefore wait for me,' declares the Lord,
　　'for the day when I rise up to seize the prey.
For my decision is to gather nations,
　　to assemble kingdoms,
to pour out upon them my indignation,
　　all my burning anger;
for in the fire of my jealousy
　　all the earth shall be consumed'" (Zeph. 3:8).

This is the dual purpose of this battle—to place Jesus on his rightful throne while bringing wicked and deceived mankind into a trap that destroys them. Ezekiel and Isaiah describe this battle, as well.

"In the latter days I will bring you against my land, that the nations may know me, when through you, O Gog, I vindicate my holiness before their eyes....On that day there shall be a great earthquake in the land of Israel. The fish of the sea and the birds of the heavens and the beasts of the field and all creeping things that creep on the ground, and all the people who are on the face of the earth, shall quake at my presence. And the mountains shall be thrown down, and the cliffs shall fall, and every wall shall tumble to the ground. I will summon a sword against Gog on all my mountains, declares the Lord God. Every man's sword will be against his brother. With pestilence and bloodshed I will enter into judgment with him, and I will rain upon him and his hordes and the many peoples who are with him torrential rains and hailstones, fire and sulfur. So I will show my greatness and my holiness and make myself known in the eyes of many nations. Then they will know that I am the Lord" (Eze. 38:16-23).

"The earth is utterly broken, the earth is split apart, the earth is violently shaken. The earth staggers like a drunken man; it sways like a hut; its transgression lies heavy upon it, and it falls, and will not rise again" (Isa. 24:19-20).

"Oh that you would rend the heavens and come down, that the mountains might quake at your presence—as when fire kindles brushwood and the fire causes water to boil—to make your name known to your adversaries, and that the nations might tremble at your presence!" (Isaiah 64:1-2).

God responds with wrath and the assurance that he laughs at the plans of the mighty. Despite what the kings of the earth may believe, Jesus rules over all nations from Zion. This rule "with a rod of iron" begins at this time but has yet to be fully realized.

With the nations gathered at Armageddon, the seventh bowl is poured out with the declaration, "It is done." This signifies the final destruction of Babylon the great. The language used here is the same as in Revelation 4:5, indicating the presence of God. The greatest earthquake in history is now released. It is one great enough to destroy the cities of the nations, move every island from its place, and fell every mountain on the earth. In addition, a plague of hail is released.

NATIONS ASSEMBLED

Throughout the course of the first six bowls, Satan through the Antichrist and the false prophet has been methodically killing those not receiving the mark and preparing for this ultimate confrontation between two very well defined groups of good and evil. The only elect remaining is Israel, who dwells securely under the protection of Jesus. Once the Antichrist's base of power is destroyed at the fifth bowl and he is forced to retreat, Israel is able to re-inhabit Jerusalem and the surrounding areas. Israel is now totally physically defenseless, as she had previously given up her weapons and army for the Antichrist's guaranteed protection, but he is now gone from the land (Dan. 11:45).

We find a similar description of these events in Ezekiel. In Chapter 38, we read that "in the latter years" Israel dwells securely (v. 8) and without walls, bars, or gates (v. 11). At that time, there will be a great earthquake (v. 19) that will be felt by all creatures throughout the earth. This earthquake will throw down the mountains and cliffs and the cities of all of the nations on earth (v. 20). Following the great earthquake, there is pestilence, including a plague of hailstones of extreme magnitude (v. 22). We find a similar description in Isaiah 24:19-20 (also Isaiah 24:19-20):

> "The earth is utterly broken, the earth is split apart, the earth is violently shaken. The earth staggers like a drunken man; it sways like a hut; its transgression lies heavy upon it, and it falls, and will not rise again."

We also find this great earthquake and its epicenter further described in Zechariah:

> "On that day his feet shall stand on the Mount of Olives that lies before Jerusalem on the east, and the Mount of Olives shall be split in two from east to west by a very wide valley, so that one half of the Mount shall move northward, and the other half southward. And you shall flee to the valley of my mountains, for the valley of the mountains shall reach to Azal. And you shall

flee as you fled from the earthquake in the days of Uzziah king of Judah. Then the Lord my God will come, and all the holy ones with him" (Zech. 14:4-5).

"The whole land shall be turned into a plain from Geba to Rimmon south of Jerusalem. But Jerusalem shall remain aloft on its site from the Gate of Benjamin to the place of the former gate, to the Corner Gate, and from the Tower of Hananel to the king's winepresses" (Zech. 14:10).

In the same context, Zechariah uses similar language as Ezekiel 38:21, speaking of the consequences for those attacking Jerusalem:

"And this shall be the plague with which the Lord will strike all the peoples that wage war against Jerusalem: their flesh will rot while they are still standing on their feet, their eyes will rot in their sockets, and their tongues will rot in their mouths. And on that day a great panic from the Lord shall fall on them, so that each will seize the hand of another, and the hand of the one will be raised against the hand of the other" (Zech. 14:12-13).

Before we see the outcome of the battle at Armageddon, John interrupts the chronology with another vision. He heightens the anticipation of final judgment upon the nations by describing another judgment that is occurring at the same time: the judgment of Babylon the great.

chapter ten

SECOND THEOLOGICAL INTERLUDE
APOSTATE CHRISTIANITY / WORLD RELIGION

Then one of the seven angels who had the seven bowls came and said to me, "Come, I will show you the judgment of the great prostitute who is seated on many waters, with whom the kings of the earth have committed sexual immorality, and with the wine of whose sexual immorality the dwellers on earth have become drunk." And he carried me away in the Spirit into a wilderness, and I saw a woman sitting on a scarlet beast that was full of blasphemous names, and it had seven heads and ten horns. The woman was arrayed in purple and scarlet, and adorned with gold and jewels and pearls, holding in her hand a golden cup full of abominations and the impurities of her sexual immorality. And on her forehead was written a name of mystery: "Babylon the great, mother of prostitutes and of earth's abominations." And I saw the woman, drunk with the blood of the saints, the blood of the martyrs of Jesus.

REVELATION 17:1-6

Here we come across the second of John's theological interludes. Earlier, in Revelation 16:19, God remembers Babylon the great. At this point, the apostle injects this interlude to provide more details on this woman before continuing the account of how she drains the cup of God's wrath.

The woman is described as a great prostitute with whom the kings of the world have committed adultery. She is elaborately adorned on the outside, but full of filthiness on the inside. As we will see, this symbolizes false religion that has seduced and corrupted all the nations of the world. The woman stands in contrast to God's elect, the undefiled bride of Christ.

This woman's origin is revealed in her name, Babylon the great. Her roots date back to the time immediately following the flood, the rise of the nation of Babylon, and the birth of the world's works-based religions. These false religions can be generally categorized as those prompting man to try to become acceptable to god(s) through good works. Over time, mutations on this theology have generated the various established religions. Despite differing interpretations of what constitutes good works, the core belief that one's relationship to God is established through works is the same in them all. It is this common belief that will allow the synchronization of the world faiths led by the false prophet. This is why in verse five Babylon the great is described as the mother of prostitutes.

It was out of this works-based system that Abraham was called to lead Israel in a true relationship with God based on faith. His faith was based on the truth that, on their own, human beings are incapable of ever being good enough to obtain a relationship with a perfect, holy God and must rely on God's provision. Abraham looked forward to a time when God, in his mercy, would provide this way. Abraham's spiritual descendents (all who would ultimately believe) realized this promise in the sacrifice of Jesus. However, Abraham's physical descendents, the Jews, had been corrupted by this religion of works and no longer worshiped God through faith nor looked to God's sacrifice for their redemption. Therefore they did not recognize Jesus as their Messiah at his first advent.

> "What shall we say, then? That Gentiles who did not pursue righteousness have attained it, that is, a righteousness that is by faith; but that Israel who pursued a law that would lead

to righteousness did not succeed in reaching that law. Why? Because they did not pursue it by faith, but as if it were based on works. They have stumbled over the stumbling stone, as it is written, 'Behold, I am laying in Zion a stone of stumbling, and a rock of offense; and whoever believes in him will not be put to shame'" (Rom. 9:30-33).

This was when people of the nations outside of Israel became Abraham's spiritual descendents. Unlike the physical nation of Israel, they rejected the religions of good works and accepted the sacrifice of Jesus for their redemption, relying on their relationship with God to save them.

What is this scarlet beast on which the woman rides? By overlaying this passage onto the prophecies of Daniel, we see that this beast is the same as Daniel's fourth beast, which is also led by the Antichrist (little horn) and has ten horns. This is the fourth beast in its governmental form, whose power extends from the first seal until its destruction at Jesus' return. The beast's scarlet color is due to the blood of the martyred saints of Jesus, who have been killed by the beast (perhaps prior to the rise of the Antichrist) under the direction of the woman.

THE SEAT OF SEVEN MOUNTAINS

"When I saw her, I marveled greatly. But the angel said to me, 'Why do you marvel? I will tell you the mystery of the woman, and of the beast with seven heads and ten horns that carries her. The beast that you saw was, and is not, and is about to rise from the bottomless pit and go to destruction. And the dwellers on earth whose names have not been written in the book of life from the foundation of the world will marvel to see the beast, because it was and is not and is to come. This calls for a mind with wisdom: the seven heads are seven mountains on which the woman is seated; they are also seven kings, five of whom have fallen, one is, the other has not yet come, and when he does come he must remain only a little while. As for the beast that was and is not, it is an eighth but it belongs to the seven, and it goes to destruction. And the ten horns that you saw are ten kings who have not yet received royal power, but they are to receive authority as kings for one hour, together with the beast. These are of one mind, and they hand over their power and authority to the beast. They will make war on the Lamb, and the Lamb will conquer them, for he is Lord of lords and King of kings, and those with him are called and chosen and faithful'" (Rev.17:6-14).

The woman symbolizes not just all of the world's false religious systems, but also the apostate church during the end times. Just as the Jews' worship of God was corrupted by the Babylonian religion of works, the Christian church has become institutionalized and corrupted by it, as well. This has occurred primarily through the adoption of Christianity as the official religion of Rome by Constantine. To gain acceptance by Rome's citizenry, Constantine integrated many of the existing religious beliefs of Rome, descended from Babylon, into the Christian faith. Where is Rome located? On top of seven hills. In fact, it's often called "the city on seven hills." Hence, in this passage, we see the representation of all false, works-based religious systems symbolized by her name. We now find this great prostitute, Babylon the great, sitting on seven mountains, revealing the relationship between this false religious system and the beast with seven heads. This prostitute has participated with the beast in martyring the elect since the fifth seal.

The apostate church exists today in various forms throughout Christendom. However, at the time of the sixth seal, there will be a great falling away and the church will join itself with other religions in the persecution and martyring of the saints. This will create the end-times institution of the apostate church. But again, this is nothing new. Throughout history, the world has witnessed nations engaging in symbiotic relationships with this system in its various forms for the power and wealth of both parties. What is new this time is that the Antichrist's government (the beast kingdom) initially provides a secular political framework for this system, although that framework, in itself, is devoid of religious allegiances. The only requirement is tolerance of all religions by all religions. Obviously, this excludes the possibility of participation by the true followers of Christ, which leads to intolerance of Christ's followers and their subsequent persecution and martyrdom.

The false prophet, using the shared works-based beliefs of these religions, syncretizes them into a one-world religion. It is only at the erection of the image of the Antichrist (the abomination of desolation) in the temple by the false prophet calling for the worship of the Antichrist that the true god of this religion is revealed.

This unified world religion is initially used by the Antichrist to provide a moral code of conduct to control the world's populous. But now, with the three spirits having completely deceived the world into worshiping the Antichrist and Satan, the need for religious control is past. This religion, once simply a means to an end for the beast, is no longer needed. It is discarded in order to totally consolidate power under the Antichrist, who ultimately has no regard for any good works at all. In the end, this false religious system is merely a prostitute whose end is destruction:

> "And the angel said to me, 'The waters that you saw, where the prostitute is seated, are peoples and multitudes and nations and languages. And the ten horns that you saw, they and the beast will hate the prostitute. They will make her desolate and naked, and devour her flesh and burn her up with fire, for God has put it into their hearts to carry out his purpose by being of one mind and handing over their royal power to the beast, until the words of God are fulfilled. And the woman that you saw is the great city that has dominion over the kings of the earth'" (Rev.17:15-18).

The woman, identified here as "the great city," reveals the relationship between this false world religion and Jerusalem. We saw at the sixth trumpet that the nations have control of Jerusalem at this time:

"Then I was given a measuring rod like a staff, and I was told, 'Rise and measure the temple of God and the altar and those who worship there, but do not measure the court outside the temple; leave that out, for it is given over to the nations, and they will trample the holy city for forty-two months'" (Rev. 11:1-2).

The covenant made by the Antichrist with Israel will include the internationalization of Jerusalem as the capital of this unified one-world religion. This will include the sharing of the Temple Mount as the court outside the temple is given over to the nations.

THE SCARLET BEAST
(Daniel's Fourth Beast Covered with the Blood of the Saints)
The King that Was, and Is Not (Sixth Head)
Five Fallen Heads, One Is (Third Head)
The Other Is Not Yet Come (Seventh Head)
An Eighth Head, but It Belongs to the Seven Heads (Sixth Head)
Ten Horns—Ten Kings to Receive Authority for One Hour

Here at the seventh bowl, we are in the middle of the series of seven leaders who will rule during the end times. We are told that five of the seven heads have fallen and "one is and one has not yet come" (v. 10). This language reveals the sequential nature of the heads.

In verse 8, we find the beast rising from the bottomless pit, where he is thrown at the fifth bowl judgment. This is how the beast was (he was in power during the fifth bowl) and is not (he is no longer in power) but is to come (he returns to power internationally at the very end).

At this point in the chronology, heads one, two, four, five and six have fallen (five have fallen, v. 10). The third head (one is, v. 10) still retains power over the portion of the original United States that remained outside of the Re-United States or retained its own leader within the Re-United States. We are told that the beast "is not" suggesting that the beast (Antichrist) has lost power and his replacement, the seventh head, is yet to come (the other that "has not yet come", v. 10). This seventh head is very short lived: "he must remain only a little while."

The reference to the "beast that was and is not, it is an eighth but it belongs to the seven" (v. 11) refers to the sixth head (sixth consecutive leader of the beast nation) who fell at the fifth bowl but who will ultimately regain power. When he does, his seat of power will no longer be over the nation as before. Instead, while the third and seventh leaders are in power, he will rise as an international star (as an eighth head/ one of the seven; Rev. 17:11). In the text, we see this as the switch in symbolism from *heads* (kings) to *horns* (nations). Unlike the seven heads, which rule sequentially, the ten horns wield their power simultaneously "for one hour, together with the beast" (v. 12). They have been together from as early as the third seal but only obtain total control at the very end. These horns are the leaders who represent the entire population of the earth. They "are of one mind, and they hand over their power and authority to the beast" (v. 13).

This unity is a result of the deceptive spirits sent out from Satan, the Antichrist, and the false prophet at the sixth bowl. Now that the elect have all been martyred and the world is united in its worship of the Antichrist, there is no further use for the woman. Eliminating her allows for complete consolidation of power by the beast.

At this time, the seat of the Antichrist's power resides over the whole earth. All the adversaries of God have united for their destruction, and the Antichrist will be revealed as the counterfeit he is. This can be seen in the contrasting descriptions of the Antichrist and Jesus:

The Antichrist (the Beast)
"…[It] was and is not and is to come"; and is about to go to destruction" (Rev. 17:8).

Jesus
"…him who is and who was and who is to come" (Rev. 1:4; 1:8, 4:8).

A graphical illustration of the beast kingdom as it changes throughout the time of the end can be found in the chart "The Beast through the Time of the End."

APOSTATE CHRISTIANITY / WORLD RELIGION
Destroyed by Beast's Ten Horns

"After this I saw another angel coming down from heaven, having great authority, and the earth was made bright with his glory. And he called out with a mighty voice, 'Fallen, fallen is Babylon the great! She has become a dwelling place for demons, a haunt for every unclean spirit, a haunt for every unclean bird, a haunt for every unclean and detestable beast. For all nations have drunk the wine of the passion of her sexual immorality, and the kings of the earth have committed immorality with her, and the merchants of the earth have grown rich from the power of her luxurious living. . . Alas! Alas! You great city, you mighty city, Babylon! For in a single hour your judgment has come'" (Rev. 18:10).

After describing the relationship between the woman and the governments of the world, including the beast, we are now given a detailed description of how integrated the woman has become with the people of the earth and its economic system. This reveals the totality to which the woman has corrupted the earth. But this woman, so spectacular in her beauty, is destroyed in spectacular fashion, as well.

As the people of the earth weep and mourn the destruction of what they value most (material goods that bring comfort), the reaction in heaven is one of great rejoicing.

"After this I heard what seemed to be the loud voice of a great multitude in heaven, crying out, 'Hallelujah! Salvation and glory and power belong to our God, for his judgments are true and just; for he has judged the great prostitute who corrupted the earth with her immorality, and has avenged on her the blood of his servants.' Once more they cried out, 'Hallelujah! The smoke from her goes up forever and ever'" (Rev. 19:1-3).

With the woman destroyed and power consolidated in the beast, we now have the beast in its final form. This form consists of two parts:

- The beast nation being led by the seventh head (seventh consecutive leader of the beast nation).

- The ten international leaders (ten horns, including the seventh head) led by the sixth head (the Antichrist), who is also considered the eighth head due to his loss of power and return.

The unification of the world against God through the deceiving spirits from the satanic trio (Satan, the beast, and the false prophet) is complete. God is now poised for their destruction.

chapter eleven

CHRIST'S SECOND COMING

Then I saw heaven opened, and behold, a white horse! The one sitting on it is called Faithful and True, and in righteousness he judges and makes war. His eyes are like a flame of fire, and on his head are many diadems, and he has a name written that no one knows but himself. He is clothed in a robe dipped in blood, and the name by which he is called is The Word of God. And the armies of heaven, arrayed in fine linen, white and pure, were following him on white horses. From his mouth comes a sharp sword with which to strike down the nations, and he will rule them with a rod of iron. He will tread the winepress of the fury of the wrath of God the Almighty. On his robe and on his thigh he has a name written, King of kings and Lord of lords.

REVELATION 19:11-16

What powerful words! At the peak of human wickedness, Jesus comes charging out of the sky as King of Kings and Lord of Lords to destroy his enemies forever. Throughout the bowls, God has been treading the winepress of his fury and wrath. Now he is about to bring this wrath to completion.

So we now return to the battle described in Revelation 16 prior to the theological interlude of Revelation 17 and 18. God has gathered the nations at Armageddon (Jezreel Valley, northern Israel), but now they move toward Jerusalem. At this point, once the nations have advanced toward Jerusalem (Joel 3:2,12), they are judged in the Valley of Jehoshaphat (Kidron Valley, Jerusalem):

"Multitudes, multitudes,
    in the valley of decision!
For the day of the Lord is near
    in the valley of decision" (Joel 3:14).

Just as prophesied concerning the day of Jezreel in Hosea 1:11 and 2:16-23, in this same valley of Jezreel that God once punished Israel for her infidelity, he now has mercy on Israel, his people, while he punishes the nations. The nations have come for battle, but they are in for a surprise. Their utter destruction awaits, completing the winepress of God. The bloodbath will be so great that blood will flow as high as a horse's bridle in the Kidron Valley (Rev. 14:20, Joel 3:2).

Here we return to the analogy of the winepress. The winepress can be viewed as being the entire nation of Israel. Armageddon (Jezreel Valley, northern Israel) is where the grapes are put in. They are tread, pressing out the juice (blood) on Israel's mountains. This blood flows through the slit (the Valley of Jehoshaphat, Kidron Valley, Jerusalem), and eventually flows down to the Dead Sea, where the blood is collected.

The order of events is interesting here. First the church is taken at the rapture. At the seventh trumpet, we see the sea of glass again, but this time we have the addition of fire, symbolizing the purification process of the church. This represents the fact that all of the works of believers not accomplished through the power of God (the Holy Spirit) are burned up and destroyed (1 Cor. 3:15).

At the same time the church is going through the purification process at the sea of glass and fire, Israel has been undergoing purification on earth through the Days of Awe leading to their atonement on Yom Kippur. By the end of the Seventieth Week when the beast's throne is plunged into darkness at the fifth bowl, their national sins have been atoned. Now it is time for the marriage supper of the Lamb, and Christ with his bride returns to earth for the destruction of evil.

MARRIAGE SUPPER OF THE LAMB

We tend to think of the marriage supper as a banquet in heaven in which all of the righteous are participating. The fact that it would actually be a bloodbath may be a surprise to some. However, the imagery is unequivocally of the feasting of birds on the wicked. While this may seem non-intuitive, what is more enjoyable to share with the Lord than the destruction of evil?

The imagery of Christ striking the nations with a rod of iron is one we have seen before. It was prophesied in Isaiah 11:4 hundreds of years earlier. Now after more than two thousand years, this ominous prophecy is coming to pass.

The description of the aftermath of God's judgment is gruesome. It will be decisive. It will be bloody, with birds of prey feeding on the carnage. These birds come at the invitation of God himself.

"Then I saw an angel standing in the sun, and with a loud voice he called to all the birds that fly directly overhead, 'Come, gather for the great supper of God, to eat the flesh of kings, the flesh of captains, the flesh of mighty men, the flesh of horses and their riders, and the flesh of all men, both free and slave, both small and great'" (Rev. 19:17-18).

This imagery is enough to churn your stomach. But this is not the first time we've seen such a picture. Ezekiel described this supper as a sacrificial feast:

"As for you, son of man, thus says the Lord God: Speak to the birds of every sort and to all beasts of the field, 'Assemble and come, gather from all around to the sacrificial feast that I am preparing for you, a great sacrificial feast on the mountains of Israel, and you shall eat flesh and drink blood. You shall eat the flesh of the mighty, and drink the blood of the princes of the earth—of rams, of lambs, and of he-goats, of bulls, all of them fat beasts of Bashan. And you shall eat fat till you are filled, and drink blood till you are drunk, at the sacrificial feast that I am preparing for you. And you shall be filled at my table with horses and charioteers, with mighty men and all kinds of warriors,' declares the Lord God" (Eze. 39:17-20).

God's enemies include the beast and the false prophet. During the battle of Armageddon, God destroys not only the nations that rage against him, but the beast and the false prophet, as well.

> "And I saw the beast and the kings of the earth with their armies gathered to make war against him who was sitting on the horse and against his army. And the beast was captured, and with it the false prophet who in its presence had done the signs by which he deceived those who had received the mark of the beast and those who worshiped its image. These two were thrown alive into the lake of fire that burns with sulfur. And the rest were slain by the sword that came from the mouth of him who was sitting on the horse, and all the birds were gorged with their flesh" (Rev. 19:19-21).

WINEPRESS OF GOD AND DANIEL'S 70ᵀᴴ WEEK COMPLETE

At this point in Revelation, Jesus has returned to destroy the beast, the false prophet, and the nations and others with them. He also binds Satan in the bottomless pit. For those who have been waiting for the vanquishing of Satan, this triumphal moment has come.

> "How you are fallen from heaven,
> O Day Star, son of Dawn!
> How you are cut down to the ground,
> you who laid the nations low!
> You said in your heart,
> 'I will ascend to heaven;

above the stars of God
I will set my throne on high;
I will sit on the mount of assembly
in the far reaches of the north;
I will ascend above the heights of the clouds;
I will make myself like the Most High.'
But you are brought down to Sheol,
to the far reaches of the pit" (Isaiah 14:12-15, emphasis mine).

This completes the treading of the winepress of God, out of which his wrath is poured (Rev. 19:15). It also ends Daniel's Seventieth Week (Dan. 9:27).

With the destruction of evil, it is no wonder that we observe a scene of such rejoicing in heaven. The earth has been harvested. The woman has been destroyed. The marriage of the bride (God's elect) has been consummated. The elect have been made pure in their glorified bodies and are wearing the same type of white robes given to the saints at the fifth seal as an assurance that God's promises will be kept. Now those promises have been fulfilled. A blessing has been given to these who have been made ready for the marriage supper. While the event itself is characterized by bloody destruction, these prophecies end with a glorious picture: a world now ruled by God.

Daniel speaks of this time in chapters two and eight. He foresees the destruction of the last of the kingdoms of Daniel's image, the feet of iron and clay, by the rock (Dan. 2:34-35). Those kingdoms are destroyed, but not by human hands (Dan. 8:25). Daniel describes the kingdom of God as a "stone not cut from human hands." Jesus, the cornerstone, destroys the nations before filling the whole earth.

"As you looked, a stone was cut out by no human hand, and it struck the image on its feet of iron and clay, and broke them in pieces. Then the iron, the clay, the bronze, the silver, and the gold, all together were broken in pieces, and became like the chaff of the summer threshing floors; and the wind carried them away, so that not a trace of them could be found. But the stone that struck the image became a great mountain and filled the whole earth" (Dan. 2:34-35).

After the destruction of God's enemies, the world will be governed by Christ. This is confirmed by the attending angel.

"And in the days of those kings the God of heaven will set up a kingdom that shall never be destroyed, nor shall the kingdom be left to another people. It shall break in pieces all these kingdoms and bring them to an end, and it shall stand forever, just as you saw that a stone was cut from a mountain by no human hand, and that it broke in pieces the iron, the bronze, the clay, the silver, and the gold. A great God has made known to the king what shall be after this. The dream is certain, and its interpretation sure" (Dan. 2:44-45).

The setting up of this eternal kingdom is also described in Daniel 7:13-14:

"I saw in the night visions, and behold, with the clouds of heaven there came one like a son of man, and he came to the Ancient of Days and was presented before him. And to him was given dominion and glory and a kingdom, that all peoples, nations, and languages should serve him; his dominion is an everlasting dominion, which shall not pass away, and his kingdom one that shall not be destroyed."

Similar promises of God's eternal kingdom can be found in Zechariah 14:5-15 and Joel 3:1-16. These prophets describe a time of utter destruction of the nations, followed by a Jerusalem that dwells securely, never again to be destroyed. They describe a time of peace, prosperity, and joy. Zechariah describes a stream of living water that flows from Jerusalem, a picture of a city inhabited by Christ. What a glorious image!

This is a picture beautifully reiterated by the Psalmist:

"There is a river whose streams make glad the city of God,
    the holy habitation of the Most High.

God is in the midst of her; she shall not be moved;
    God will help her when morning dawns.
The nations rage, the kingdoms totter;
    he utters his voice, the earth melts.
The Lord of hosts is with us;
    the God of Jacob is our fortress.
Selah

Come, behold the works of the Lord,
    how he has brought desolations on the earth.
He makes wars cease to the end of the earth;
    he breaks the bow and shatters the spear;
    he burns the chariots with fire.
'Be still, and know that I am God.
    I will be exalted among the nations,
    I will be exalted in the earth!'
The Lord of hosts is with us;
    the God of Jacob is our fortress.
Selah" (Psalm 46:4-11).

THOUSAND-YEAR REIGN OF CHRIST
Feast of Tabernacles (Booths)

Earlier we discussed how God's end-times plan fulfills the ancient feasts of Israel. This culminates with the Feast of Tabernacles, which coincides with the thousand-year reign of Christ. It is at this point that this feast is fulfilled and we see the thousand-year reign introduced.

> "Then I saw an angel coming down from heaven, holding in his hand the key to the bottomless pit and a great chain. And he seized the dragon, that ancient serpent, who is the devil and Satan, and bound him for a thousand years, and threw him into the pit, and shut it and sealed it over him, so that he might not deceive the nations any longer, until the thousand years were ended. After that he must be released for a little while" (Rev. 20:1-3).

It is also at this time that we see fulfillment of Daniel 9:24, the "anointing of the most holy place," in which King Jesus will physically reign upon the throne of David in Jerusalem.

In verse six, we are introduced to the concept of the one thousand years. Commonly called "the millennial reign," this period brings in a time of temporary global peace and prosperity for the earth and specifically for Israel. (It is a temporary peace because it is ended by the release of Satan from the pit in preparation for his final destruction.) But under the iron rule of Christ, it is also a time of continuing judgment upon the nations. Zechariah writes that all who survive Christ's return will go up year after year to worship the King, the Lord of hosts, and to keep the Feast of Booths (Zech. 14:16-21, Deut. 16:13-15). If they do not go, there will be consequences, such as plagues and the withholding of rain.

This will be a time of prosperity for faithful Jerusalem. It will be a time when God's favor rests on them so that they, along with the entire world, will know that they are his.

"So you shall know that I am the Lord your God, who dwells in Zion, my holy mountain. And Jerusalem shall be holy, and strangers shall never again pass through it. And in that day the mountains shall drip sweet wine, and the hills shall flow with milk, and all the streambeds of Judah shall flow with water; and a fountain shall come forth from the house of the Lord and water the Valley of Shittim. Egypt shall become a desolation and Edom a desolate wilderness, for the violence done to the people of Judah, because they have shed innocent blood in their land. But Judah shall be inhabited forever, and Jerusalem to all generations. I will avenge their blood, blood I have not avenged, for the Lord dwells in Zion" (Joel 3:17-21).

Ezekiel, too, writes of this period using language unmistakable in its beauty.

"You shall dwell in the land that I gave to your fathers, and you shall be my people, and I will be your God. And I will deliver you from all your uncleannesses. And I will summon the grain and make it abundant and lay no famine upon you. I will make the fruit of the tree and the increase of the field abundant, that you may never again suffer the disgrace of famine among the nations....Thus says the Lord God: On the day that I cleanse you from all your iniquities, I will cause the cities to be inhabited, and the waste places shall be rebuilt. And the land that was desolate shall be tilled, instead of being the desolation that it was in the sight of all who passed by. And they will say, 'This land that was desolate has become like the garden of Eden, and the waste and desolate and ruined cities are now fortified and inhabited.' Then the nations that are left all around you shall know that I am the Lord; I have rebuilt the ruined places and replanted that which was desolate. I am the Lord; I have spoken, and I will do it" (Eze. 36:28-36).

The language used to describe the millennial period is truly glorious. I recommend that you take the time to read passages such as Ezekiel 37:24-28, which describes faithful Israel ruled by Christ under a covenant of peace, and Ezekiel 39:25-29, which talks of God's restoration of Israel and vindication of his people before the nations. The entirety of Ezekiel 40 through 48 provides a beautiful portrayal of God's faithfulness to his people and his covenant during this time. Other passages include Amos 9:11-15, Zephaniah 3:9-20, Zechariah 8:1-17, and Isaiah 11:1-10. All of these prophets describe a period in which Christ dwells physically with his people and brings such peace that even the lion will lay down with the lamb.

"The wolf shall dwell with the lamb, and the leopard shall lie down with the young goat, and the calf and the lion and the fattened calf together; and a little child shall lead them. The cow and the bear shall graze; their young shall lie down together; and the lion shall eat straw like the ox. The nursing child shall play over the hole of the cobra, and the weaned child shall put his hand on the adder's den. They shall not hurt or destroy in all my holy mountain; for the earth shall be full of the knowledge of the Lord as the waters cover the sea. In that day the root of Jesse, who shall stand as a signal for the peoples—of him shall the nations inquire, and his resting place shall be glorious" (Isa. 11:6-10).

All of this is the ultimate fulfillment of the last of the fall feasts of the Lord, the Feast of Tabernacles. This fits precisely the pattern given in Deuteronomy 16:13-14: "You shall keep the Feast of Booths seven days, when you have gathered in the produce from your threshing floor and your winepress. You shall rejoice in your feast."

As we have discussed, the harvest of the earth began on the Feast of Trumpets with the gathering of the grain (the rapture) and the gathering of the winepress (the grape harvest). The grain harvest extends to Israel with Israel's atonement on Yom Kippur. With the culmination of the grape harvest at Jesus' second coming, the Feast of Tabernacles (Feast of Booths), a time of great rejoicing is begun. During the end times, this rejoicing, however, is not for the season's agricultural harvest but for the great harvest of souls cultivated throughout the age. So not only do we see the pattern of Deuteronomy 16:13-14 revealed here, but also the pattern of the fall feasts: Trumpets, Yom Kippur, and Tabernacles (Booths).

Since the announcement "the kingdom of the world has become the kingdom of our Lord and of his Christ" (Rev. 11:15) at the blowing of the seventh trumpet, we have experienced God's unrestrained wrath on unrepentant mankind. Now, with the subjugation of evil, we enter into a time when the order of this age (in which the selfish dominate the selfless) is reversed. Here in Revelation, we see the fulfillment of the prophecies both of the Old Testament prophets, who pointed to the coming King, and the words of Jesus himself:

"But the meek shall inherit the land and delight themselves in abundant peace" (Ps. 37:11).

"Blessed are the meek, for they shall inherit the earth" (Matt. 5:5).

What characterizes this age is the peace that comes from the ability of the selfless to rule the selfish by force, made possible by Christ's rule with a rod of iron (Psalm 2:9, Rev. 2:27; 12:5; 19:15). This restraint of evil is reflected in Satan's incarceration in the bottomless pit.

Man's sinful (selfish) nature remains. So does the curse, since people still experience death. However, man's nature is restrained to such a degree that a clear picture of what life will be like without this nature, which will come during the new heaven and new earth, is revealed to everyone. Despite the ability to experience this peace and return to the harmony of nature's order, mankind still chooses to return to rebellion upon the release of Satan, exposing the true extent of their depravity.

> "For if, after they have escaped the defilements of the world through the knowledge of our Lord and Savior Jesus Christ, they are again entangled in them and overcome, the last state has become worse for them than the first. For it would have been better for them never to have known the way of righteousness than after knowing it to turn back from the holy commandment delivered to them. What the true proverb says has happened to them: 'The dog returns to its own vomit, and the sow, after washing herself, returns to wallow in the mire'" (2 Peter 2:20-22).

So we return to Revelation 20:

> "Then I saw thrones, and seated on them were those to whom the authority to judge was committed. Also I saw the souls of those who had been beheaded for the testimony of Jesus and for the word of God, and those who had not worshiped the beast or its image and had not received its mark on their foreheads or their hands. They came to life and reigned with Christ for a thousand years. The rest of the dead did not come to life until the thousand years were ended. This is the first resurrection. Blessed and holy is the one who shares in the first resurrection! Over such the second death has no power, but

they will be priests of God and of Christ, and they will reign with him for a thousand years" (Rev. 20:4-6).

Now that we've seen the glory of the millennial period, we understand why this is such a special blessing for those who endure the reign of the Antichrist and do not take his mark. While this special group of believers may be martyred for their faithfulness, God rewards them with a position of great honor and leadership. Now that Christ has taken his rightful position of kingship over the earth, they will rule and reign with him during this time of incredible blessing.

"The scepter shall not depart from Judah, nor the ruler's staff from between his feet, until tribute comes to him; and to him shall be the obedience of the peoples" (Gen. 49:10).

This special group of God's elect, those participating in the first resurrection, come out of the time following the seventh trumpet (harvest of the earth/rapture) and extending to the third bowl. It does not include any of the remnant of Israel, since they are under Jesus' protection during this period and are therefore still alive at the beginning of the thousand-year reign.

THE LAST GREAT DAY
Eighth Day of the Feast of Tabernacles

"For seven days you shall present food offerings to the Lord. On the eighth day you shall hold a holy convocation [the Feast of Tabernacles] and present a food offering to the Lord. It is a solemn assembly; you shall not do any ordinary work" (Lev. 23:36).

"On the last day of the feast, the great day, Jesus stood up and cried out, 'If anyone thirsts, let him come to me and drink'" (John 7:37).

The Feast of Tabernacles concludes at this place in the chronology, and in John's gospel, we see a very important confirmation of that. In this verse, Jesus very clearly ties the end of the feast with his presence with the people as the fount of living water. Indeed, in the chronology of

Revelation, the Feast of Tabernacles ends immediately before Revelation 21 and 22, where we see the image of Jesus as the living water woven powerfully throughout:

> "And he said to me, "It is done! I am the Alpha and the Omega, the beginning and the end. To the thirsty I will give from the spring of the water of life without payment" (Rev. 21:6).

> "Then the angel showed me the river of the water of life, bright as crystal, flowing from the throne of God and of the Lamb" (Rev. 22:1).

The tie is made even stronger when one considers that John penned both the gospel of John and the book of Revelation.

Also called "the last great day," the solemn assembly on the eighth day of the Feast of Tabernacles foreshadows a two-fold event: the great white throne judgment of God and the preparation for the new heaven and the new earth, a time when Jesus will dwell with his people.

In fulfillment of this last great day, however, the peace that characterizes the thousand-year reign must be broken. From the beginning of the thousand years until this time, Satan has been bound in the pit, but he has not yet been destroyed. At the end of the thousand years, Satan is given one more opportunity to deceive the nations in preparation for the final judgment.

> "And when the thousand years are ended, Satan will be released from his prison and will come out to deceive the nations that are at the four corners of the earth, Gog and Magog, to gather them for battle; their number is like the sand of the sea" (Rev. 20:7-8).

How wicked is the heart of man! Despite the peaceful rule of Jesus for one thousand years, once again the nations fall to the deception of Satan, rebel, and follow Satan's lead to seek independence from God. This is the final testimony in God's case against mankind and illustrates the total depravity of mankind as God prepares to judge them and turn them over to the desires of their hearts.

Perhaps this is why this passage reads as if God is making a legal case.

By this time, man will have exhausted every means for excuse. Man can no longer say, "I would have come to you if you would have created the circumstances that were ideal. Under those conditions, I surely would have followed you. I surely would have known what it means to have a relationship with you." The millennial reign, followed by the rapid descent into rebellion, takes that argument away. Jesus ruled for one thousand years. Yet given the opportunity, even under ideal conditions, mankind fell away again. Every age gives mankind a different approach to God. Every time, man fails. This is the last perfect situation.

Ultimately, however, just as in the previous battle, the end of Satan and his angels is sure.

"And they marched up over the broad plain of the earth and surrounded the camp of the saints and the beloved city, but fire came down from heaven and consumed them, and the devil who had deceived them was thrown into the lake of fire and sulfur where the beast and the false prophet were, and they will be tormented day and night forever and ever" (Rev. 20:9-10).

At this point, God brings his final judgment upon the earth. The books are opened and the final judgments read.

"Then I saw a great white throne and him who was seated on it. From his presence earth and sky fled away, and no place was found for them. And I saw the dead, great and small, standing before the throne, and books were opened. Then another book was opened, which is the book of life. And the dead were judged by what was written in the books, according to what they had done. And the sea gave up the dead who were in it, Death and Hades gave up the dead who were in them, and they were judged, each one of them, according to what they had done. Then Death and Hades were thrown into the lake of fire. This is the second death, the lake of fire. And if anyone's name was not found written in the book of life, he was thrown into the lake of fire" (Rev. 20:11-15).

This reminds us of Daniel's second vision:

"As I looked, thrones were placed, and the Ancient of Days took his seat; his clothing was white as snow, and the hair of his head like pure wool; his throne was fiery flames; its wheels were burning fire. A stream of fire issued and came out from before him; a thousand thousands served him, and ten thousand times ten thousand stood before him; the court sat in judgment, and the books were opened. I looked then because of the sound of the great words that the horn was speaking. And as I looked, the beast was killed, and its body destroyed and given over to be burned with fire. As for the rest of the beasts, their dominion was taken away, but their lives were prolonged for a season and a time" (Dan. 7:9-12).

Daniel's vision coincides perfectly with Revelation 20, the time of the resurrection of the dead in the final judgment.

"And many of those who sleep in the dust of the earth shall awake, some to everlasting life, and some to shame and everlasting contempt. And those who are wise shall shine like the brightness of the sky above; and those who turn many to righteousness, like the stars forever and ever" (Dan.12:2-3).

This is the second resurrection, the resurrection of those in Christ out of the thousand-year reign of Christ and those lost throughout history.

At this time, we see the fulfillment of promises such as those found in 1 Corinthians 15:24-29: "Then comes the end, when he delivers the kingdom to God the Father after destroying every rule and every authority and power." And John 5:19-30: "So Jesus said to them… 'The Father judges no one, but has given all judgment to the Son, that all may honor the Son, just as they honor the Father… Do not marvel at this, for an hour is coming when all who are in the tombs will hear his voice.'"

We also see a fulfillment of Malachi 4:1-3:

"For behold, the day is coming, burning like an oven, when all the arrogant and all evildoers will be stubble. The day that is coming shall set them ablaze, says the Lord of hosts, so that it will leave them neither root nor branch. But for you who fear my name, the sun of righteousness shall rise with healing in its wings. You shall go out leaping like calves from the stall. And you shall tread down the wicked, for they will be ashes under the soles of your feet, on the day when I act, says the Lord of hosts."

We read about this final judgment in Matthew 25, as well:

"When the Son of Man comes in his glory, and all the angels with him, then he will sit on his glorious throne. Before him will be gathered all the nations, and he will separate people one from another as a shepherd separates the sheep from the goats. And he will place the sheep on his right, but the goats on the left. Then the King will say to those on his right, 'Come, you who are blessed by my Father, inherit the kingdom prepared for you from the foundation of the world. For I was hungry and you gave me food, I was thirsty and you gave me drink, I was a stranger and you welcomed me, I was naked and you clothed me, I was sick and you visited me, I was in prison and you came to me.' Then the righteous will answer him, saying, 'Lord, when did we see you hungry and feed you, or thirsty and give you drink? And when did we see you a stranger and welcome you, or naked and clothe you? And when did we see you sick or in prison and visit you?' And the King will answer them, 'Truly, I say to you, as you did it to one of the least of these my brothers, you did it to me.' Then he will say to those on his left, 'Depart from me, you cursed, into the eternal fire prepared for the devil and his angels. For I was hungry and you gave me no food, I was thirsty and you gave me no drink, I was a stranger and you did not welcome me, naked and you did not clothe me, sick and in prison and you did not visit me.' Then they also will answer, saying, 'Lord, when did we see you hungry or thirsty or a stranger or naked or sick or in prison, and did not minister to you?' Then he will answer them, saying, 'Truly, I say to you, as you did not do it to one of the least of these, you did not do it to me.' And these will go away into eternal punishment, but the righteous into eternal life" (Matt. 25:31-46).

At this time, the King of Kings will finally be vindicated.

chapter twelve

NEW HEAVEN, NEW EARTH, NEW JERUSALEM

A t this point, we have come to the end of the book of Revelation. Here God gives us a glimpse of the glory that awaits those who are faithful, whether they live to see the terror of the Antichrist or go to be with the Lord before then. It is a glimpse of the magnificence of the promise to come. For these faithful, God recreates the heaven and the earth and brings forth splendor beyond that which existed even before the fall of man. For now man's love for God mirrors God's love for man. This is made possible only through the expression of sacrificial love in Christ, revealing the necessity of the fall and how God used evil in executing his plan to create this love.

"Then I saw a new heaven and a new earth, for the first heaven and the first earth had passed away, and the sea was no more. And I saw the holy city, new Jerusalem, coming down out of heaven from God, prepared as a bride adorned for her husband. And I heard a loud voice from the throne saying, 'Behold, the dwelling place of God is with man. He will dwell with them, and they will be his people, and God himself will be with them as their God. He will wipe away every tear from their eyes, and death shall be no more, neither shall there be mourning, nor crying, nor pain anymore, for the former things have passed away.' And he who was seated on the throne said, 'Behold, I am making all things new.' Also he said, 'Write this down, for these words are trustworthy and true'" (Rev. 21:1-5).

The same angel who once brought the final plagues now shows the apostle John the glories awaiting the bride of Christ. He describes the New Jerusalem adorned with jewels, laid on the foundation of the twelve apostles and entered through the gates of the twelve tribes of Israel.

"Then came one of the seven angels who had the seven bowls full of the seven last plagues and spoke to me, saying, 'Come, I will show you the Bride, the wife of the Lamb.' And he carried me away in the Spirit to a great, high mountain, and showed me the holy city Jerusalem coming down out of heaven from God, having the glory of God, its radiance like a most rare jewel, like a jasper, clear as crystal. It had a great, high wall, with twelve gates, and at the gates twelve angels, and on the gates the names of the twelve tribes of the sons of Israel were inscribed—on the east three gates, on the north three gates, on the south three gates, and on the west three gates. And the wall of the city had twelve foundations, and on them were the twelve names of the twelve apostles of the Lamb" (Rev. 21:6-14).

The beauty of this city defies description. Yet this indescribable glory will be the home of the faithful bride:

"The wall was built of jasper, while the city was pure gold, clear as glass. The foundations of the wall of the city were adorned with every kind of jewel. The first was jasper, the second sapphire, the third agate, the fourth emerald, the fifth onyx, the sixth carnelian, the seventh chrysolite, the eighth beryl, the ninth topaz, the tenth chrysoprase, the eleventh jacinth, the twelfth amethyst. And the twelve gates were twelve pearls, each of the gates made of a single pearl, and the street of the city was pure gold, transparent as glass. And I saw no temple in the city, for its temple is the Lord God the Almighty and the Lamb. And the city has no need of sun or moon to shine on it, for the glory of God gives it light, and its lamp is the Lamb. By its light will the nations walk, and the kings of the earth will bring their glory into it, and its gates will never be shut by day—and there will be no night there. They will bring into it the glory and the honor of the nations. But nothing unclean will ever enter it, nor anyone who does what is detestable or false, but only those who are written in the Lamb's book of life" (Rev. 21:19-27).

The old heaven and earth have passed away, but God's Word has not (Matt. 5:18; 24:25). All prophecy has been fulfilled. In the New Jerusalem, we see the complete bride of Christ, which includes all of the elect, both Israel and the church (both Old Testament and New), dwelling with God.

"For behold, I create new heavens and a new earth, and the former things shall not be remembered or come into mind. But be glad and rejoice forever in that which I create; for behold, I create Jerusalem to be a joy, and her people to be a gladness" (Isa. 65:17-19).

At this time, truly we can say that the kingdom has been delivered to God the Father (1 Cor. 15:24).

"Then the angel showed me the river of the water of life, bright as crystal, flowing from the throne of God and of the Lamb through the middle of the street of the city; also, on either side of the river, the tree of life with its twelve kinds of fruit, yielding its fruit each month. The leaves of the tree were for the healing of the nations. No longer will there be anything accursed, but the throne of God and of the Lamb will be in it, and his servants will worship him. They will see his face, and his name will be on their foreheads. And night will be no more. They will need no light of lamp or sun, for the Lord God will be their light, and they will reign forever and ever. And he said to me, 'These words are trustworthy and true. And the Lord, the God of the spirits of the prophets, has sent his angel to show his servants what must soon take place'" (Rev. 22:1-6).

In the last chapter of Revelation, John continues to share with the reader the joys of blessedness that await those who are faithful to Christ. Not only will the New Jerusalem be a place of beauty, but it will be a place where evil has been abolished and the faithful dwell in the presence of Christ for eternity. What a promise for those who are about to endure the greatest persecution in history! What a tremendous motivator to faithfulness! It will all be worth it in the end. John concludes this description with a reminder of the faithfulness of God: "These words are trustworthy and true" (v. 6).

But there is a warning here, too. Through the apostle John, Jesus tells us that these days are rapidly coming upon us. There is no time to waste. We must be prepared: "Behold, I am coming soon, bringing my recompense with me, to repay everyone for what he has done. I am the Alpha and the Omega, the first and the last, the beginning and the end" (Rev. 22:12-13).

Jesus repeats this warning in three other places:

"Behold, I am coming soon. Blessed is the one who keeps the words of the prophecy of this book" (v. 7).

"He said to me, 'Do not seal up the words of the prophecy of this book, for the time is near'" (v. 10).

"He who testifies to these things says, 'Surely I am coming soon.'" (v. 20)

These verses remind us of the warning given two thousand years ago as Jesus stood upon the Mount of Olives:

"From the fig tree learn its lesson: as soon as its branch becomes tender and puts out its leaves, you know that summer is near. So also, when you see these things taking place, you know that he is near, at the very gates. Truly, I say to you, this generation will not pass away until all these things take place. Heaven and earth will pass away, but my words will not pass away" (Mark 13:28-30).

"And he told them a parable: 'Look at the fig tree, and all the trees. As soon as they come out in leaf, you see for yourselves and know that the summer is already near. So also, when you see these things taking place, you know that the kingdom of God is near. Truly, I say to you, this generation will not pass away until all has taken place. Heaven and earth will pass away, but my words will not pass away'" (Luke 21:29-33).

Here we see Jesus, speaking about "these things" (the events of the time of the end), state that the generation alive at the time of the beginning of the fulfillment of these things will not pass away until they have all taken place. Therefore, once the first seal is broken, all the events prophesied in Revelation will come to pass within a single generation, with the prophesied events (like birth pains [Matt. 24:8]) occurring with ever-increasing frequency and intensity. The actual length of a generation is up for debate. However, we know that from the fifth trumpet to Jesus' second coming is seven years and five months. Therefore we can conclude that, since these events will transpire more rapidly than the events from the first seal to the fourth trumpet, the entire period we call "the time of the end" is at least fifteen years. It will likely be longer, but that is as accurate as we can be.

The times have changed, but the warnings have not. In fact, as we see prophecy fulfilled before our very eyes, those warnings carry even greater urgency. These warnings are so critical that John is told to write the sternest possible admonition against tampering with the book of Revelation so that these warnings may be preserved for believers and unbelievers alike.

"I warn everyone who hears the words of the prophecy of this book: if anyone adds to them, God will add to him the plagues described in this book, and if anyone takes away from the words of the book of this prophecy, God will take away his share in the tree of life and in the holy city, which are described in this book" (Rev. 22:18-19).

Just as he did two thousand years ago, Jesus testifies of his own faithfulness and to the certainty of the fulfillment of this prophecy. The fulfillment of his words is so certain, in fact, that Jesus testifies of himself: "He who testifies to these things says, 'Surely I am coming soon.' Amen. Come, Lord Jesus!" (Rev. 22:20).

WHAT'S IT MEAN FOR YOU?

What does all this mean for you? Throughout the book of Revelation, the theme is the same as throughout all Scripture: a call to repentance with the promise of an eternal relationship with God the Father through the sacrifice of his son, Jesus. This relationship is so important, so secure, that it carries us through every trial and tribulation, even if that should be unto death at the hands of the Antichrist.

God loves each one of us, including those perishing in the depths of sin. That's why, before God releases his wrath on rebellious mankind, he provides ample opportunity for repentance. Each time this opportunity is not taken, however, God's wrath increases. Ultimately, this results in eternal separation from him. God's wrath is kindled out of love and a desire for relationship with those who deserve only death and separation. But this love requires justice, a separation of those who love him from those who don't.

If you are not counted among the believers in Christ, the call could not be clearer. God's wrath begins to be poured out first in the trumpet judgments, then in full strength during the bowls, and ultimately in his eternal wrath at the final judgment. The sooner you repent and turn to God, the less of God's earthly judgment you will endure. There is much reward promised to those who repent—not just escaping his temporal wrath but also an eternal existence with a perfect relationship with God that translates into perfect, selfless relationships unifying all who love him.

Today you chose: acceptance of God's love and an eternal relationship with him or rejection of that love leading to God's wrath and eternal separation.

The apostle Peter warned against the dangers of becoming complacent. He knew that it is easy to say, "Jesus has been delayed all this time. Why do I need to worry about it now?" That's why he warned directly of this and offered dire consequences for taking his delay as a false sense of security.

"For they deliberately overlook this fact, that the heavens existed long ago, and the earth was formed out of water and through water by the word of God, and that by means of these the world that then existed was deluged with water and perished. But by the same word the heavens and earth that now exist are stored up for fire, being kept until the day of judgment and destruction of the ungodly. But do not overlook this one fact, beloved, that with the Lord one day is as a thousand years, and a thousand years as one day. The Lord is not slow to fulfill his promise as some count slowness, but is patient toward you, not wishing that any should perish, but that all should reach repentance. But the day of the Lord will come like a thief, and then the heavens will pass away with a roar, and the heavenly bodies will be burned up and dissolved, and the earth and the works that are done on it will be exposed. Since all these things are thus to be dissolved, what sort of people ought you to be in lives of holiness and godliness, waiting for and hastening the coming of the day of God, because of which the heavens will be set on fire and dissolved, and the heavenly bodies will melt as they burn! But according to his promise we are waiting for new heavens and a new earth in which righteousness dwells" (2 Peter 3:5-13).

For the ungodly, the future is grim. For God's elect, the promise is glory. For those still alive during the end times and holding onto their faith even unto death, the book of Revelation provides the promise of peace. Those saints carry the knowledge that God is in control and that he is executing his plan without fail. While they can count on receiving the full force of mankind's wrath for holding true, they can also count on escaping God's wrath and receiving eternal blessings for doing so. For those whose belief is in Jesus, his grace is sufficient to endure all things.

"Grace to you and peace from him who is and who was and who is to come, and from the seven spirits who are before his throne" (Rev. 1:4).

BACKGROUND FROM DANIEL

As the events of Revelation unfold, we are viewing in modern context people, places, and events that were foretold hundreds of years earlier by the prophet Daniel. By turning our attention to the book after his name, we are given the background to understand who these individuals are, their relationship to others on the national stage, and their broader role in end-times prophecy. It is in Daniel that we get to know these individuals. In Revelation, this helps us understand what they do.

Daniel records multiple visions given to him during Israel's Babylonian captivity. In the first vision, Daniel saw what had previously been shown to Nebuchadnezzar, the king of Babylon, in a dream:

> "You saw, O king, and behold, a great image. This image, mighty and of exceeding brightness, stood before you, and its appearance was frightening. The head of this image was of fine gold, its chest and arms of silver, its middle and thighs of bronze, its legs of iron, its feet partly of iron and partly of clay" (Dan. 2:31-33).

Notice that Nebuchadnezzar did not tell Daniel his dream. First God gave Daniel the supernatural insight to know the content of King Nebuchadnezzar's dream. Then once Daniel was given this revelation,

God supplied him with the interpretation. That Daniel knew the content of Nebuchadnezzar's dream without being told tells us that both the dream and the interpretation are from God. Thus, as Daniel tells the king, "its interpretation [is] sure" (Daniel 2:45).

The dream described four powerful kingdoms that would rule throughout history and be used by God to bring punishment upon (and ultimately repentance to) Israel. The head of gold represents Nebuchadnezzar's kingdom. The chest and arms of silver represent the kingdom of the Medes and Persians, which destroyed Nebuchadnezzar's kingdom and took its place as preeminent on the world stage. The Medes and Persians were conquered by Greece, represented by the middle and thighs of bronze. We are particularly interested in the fourth kingdom, which both conquered Greece in history past and will experience a revival at the time of the end:

> "And there shall be a fourth kingdom, strong as iron, because iron breaks to pieces and shatters all things. And like iron that crushes, it shall break and crush all these. And as you saw the feet and toes, partly of potter's clay and partly of iron, it shall be a divided kingdom, but some of the firmness of iron shall be in it, just as you saw iron mixed with the soft clay. And as the toes of the feet were partly iron and partly clay, so the kingdom shall be partly strong and partly brittle. As you saw the iron mixed with soft clay, so they will mix with one another in marriage, but they will not hold together, just as iron does not mix with clay. And in the days of those kings the God of heaven will set up a kingdom that shall never be destroyed, nor shall the kingdom be left to another people. It shall break in pieces all these kingdoms and bring them to an end, and it shall stand forever, just as you saw that a stone was cut from a mountain by no human hand, and that it broke in pieces the iron, the bronze, the clay, the silver, and the gold. A great God has made known to the king what shall be after this. The dream is certain, and its interpretation sure" (Dan. 2:40-45).

This fourth kingdom is the kingdom in power at the time of the end. In Revelation 17, we see it described as the beast kingdom. This kingdom is illustrated as having ten horns (or ten toes, Daniel 2:42) representing ten nations or regional governments in an alliance at the time of the end. But God does not allow these earthly kingdoms to triumph. In the end, and described in much more powerful detail in Revelation, we see these kingdoms replaced by one final kingdom—God's (Dan. 2:40-45, Dan. 7:26-27, Dan. 8:25, Dan. 11:45, Rev. 17:11).

The latter portion of the interpretation is critically important to the study of the end times. This is because the imagery of the "stone cut out of the mountain without hands" represents Christ's eternal kingdom, which destroys God's enemies and fills the earth. This tells us that the fourth kingdom is the last and final earthly kingdom before God's kingdom is established. If the fourth and final kingdom is followed by God's eternal kingdom, then by implication, it will exist during the end times. Therefore, the more we understand this fourth kingdom, the more we will understand the events described in Revelation.

Let's look at another prophecy given to Daniel some years later. At this time, Daniel was given what he called a "night vision," one that dealt with four beasts. As with the vision in Daniel 2, we are concerned with the fourth of these beasts since it, too, represents the last and final earthly kingdom before God's kingdom is established. Daniel described the fourth beast as follows:

> "After this I saw in the night visions, and behold, a fourth beast, terrifying and dreadful and exceedingly strong. It had great iron teeth; it devoured and broke in pieces and stamped what was left with its feet. It was different from all the beasts that were before it, and it had ten horns" (Dan. 7:7).

With this dream, the interpretation was given to Daniel by what we can presume to be an angel:

> "Thus he said: 'As for the fourth beast, there shall be a fourth kingdom on earth, which shall be different from all the

kingdoms, and it shall devour the whole earth, and trample it down, and break it to pieces. As for the ten horns, out of this kingdom ten kings shall arise, and another shall arise after them. But the court shall be seated, and they shall take away his dominion, to consume and destroy it forever. Then the kingdom and dominion, and the greatness of the kingdoms under the whole heaven shall be given to the people, the saints of the Most High. His kingdom is an everlasting kingdom and all dominions shall serve and obey Him'" (Dan. 7:23-27).

As with the previous vision, this one ends with the fourth earthly kingdom being destroyed and replaced with God's eternal kingdom (Dan 7:26-27). Thus these two dreams foretell the same basic events—the demise of the final kingdom in power at the time of the end. This is the same time period described in Revelation 13 and 17. These ten horns of Daniel's fourth beast represent national or regional world leaders (or "kings") that play visible and identifiable roles we discuss in detail throughout this book.

The next piece of the puzzle is a third vision given to Daniel two years later:

"I raised my eyes and saw, and behold, a ram standing on the bank of the canal. It had two horns, and both horns were high, but one was higher than the other, and the higher one came up last. I saw the ram charging westward and northward and southward. No beast could stand before him, and there was no one who could rescue from his power. He did as he pleased and became great. As I was considering, behold, a male goat came from the west across the face of the whole earth, without touching the ground. And the goat had a conspicuous horn between his eyes. He came to the ram with the two horns, which I had seen standing on the bank of the canal, and he ran at him in his powerful wrath. I saw him come close to the ram, and he was enraged against him and struck the ram and broke his two horns. And the ram had no power to stand before him, but he cast him down to the ground and trampled on him. And there was no one who could rescue the ram from his power" (Dan. 8:3-7).

As with Daniel's other prophecies, the imagery of animals and horns relates to powers, both national and individual, at the time of the end. In this case, the imagery is of a conspicuous horn (or "notable horn" in some translations) that represents a political entity of great importance that arises during the end times.

Many have interpreted Daniel's ram and goat prophecy as being fulfilled by Alexander the Great at the battle of Gaugamela in 331 B.C. (and ultimately with the destruction of Persepolis in 330 B.C). However, as discussed in the commentary on the second seal, this fulfillment can only be viewed as figurative. This leaves its literal fulfillment to the time of the end. This is confirmed by the angel Gabriel, who gives the interpretation:

"He said, 'Behold, I will make known to you what shall be at the latter end of the indignation, for it refers to the *appointed time of the end*'" (Dan. 8:19, emphasis mine).

The clear time marker ("the time of the end") occurs not only in Daniel 8:19 but in Daniel 8:17, as well:

"As he came near the place where I was standing, I was terrified and fell prostrate. 'Son of man,' he said to me, 'understand that the vision *concerns the time of the end*'" (emphasis mine).

What are these prophecies trying to tell us? Regardless of the imagery used, this fourth and final earthly kingdom is described as having seven heads and ten horns (Rev. 13:1; Dan. 7:7). In biblical prophecy, horns are commonly understood to be kingdoms, or in modern language, nations or possibly regional governments. Heads are commonly understood to be kings. In modern terms, we could see them as national leaders. In this case, these leaders are commonly understood to be chronological—leaders who reign over this final earthly "kingdom" over time. That we can refer to this beast as the beast nation distinguishes it from the beast, an individual (Revelation 13). So when we say "the beast kingdom" or "the beast nation," we are referring to the beast of Revelation 17 and also to the fourth and final earthly kingdom described in Daniel 2 and Daniel 7.

By taking the first of the seven leaders of the beast nation and using the time markers of Revelation 17 overlaid with description of the changes in the horns in Daniel 7:8, a timeline emerges that places the seven leaders within the time of the end beginning with the first seal.

What do we know about the beast kingdom? We know that it has seven heads (or leaders) and ten horns. Because the horns have authority with the beast for "one hour," and because they make war with the beast and all together are conquered by the Lamb (Rev.17:12-14), we know that unlike the national leaders who rule in succession (Rev. 17:10-11), the ten horns exist simultaneously. This tells us that the fourth kingdom has a governmental form that exists in an international (ten horns) as well as a national (seven heads) form.

Putting all of this together, we see the final world kingdom at the time of the end characterized as follows:

- The kingdom originates from the "notable horn" of the goat kingdom (Daniel 8) from which its predominate leader emerges.

- The seven-headed beast represents a "beast nation" with seven sequential kings or leaders, with each taking his turn throughout the time of the end (Revelation 13, 17).

- The 10-horned "beast alliance," of which this beast nation is a part, is made up partly of iron and partly of clay (Daniel 7). Iron represents the strength of leadership of the heads of the beast nation and clay represents the weakness of the ten-nation international alliance. Iron also symbolizes the West, an extension of the Roman Empire in modern times.

It is from the beast nation from which, except for Jesus himself, emerges the most famous character from Revelation. This is the Antichrist. The term "Antichrist" is not used in Revelation. Rather he is seen as the sixth head on the beast nation. In Daniel, he is known as "the little horn" (Dan. 7:7-8; 8:9). According to Scripture, the Antichrist has primarily a political role. He emerges from one of the four nations that arises from the notable horn (Dan. 8:8), which we have identified as being most likely (but not definitively) the United States. This is the nation from which the Antichrist emerges and the nation that leads the 10-nation beast alliance arising during the end times. Ultimately, the Antichrist uses his power to subdue three of the four nations (Dan. 7:8).

Although we see the Antichrist here as the little horn, in the chronology of Revelation we don't actually see him emerge until the sixth trumpet. By the time he arises, we've already seen the rise of five "heads" in these Danielic prophecies—the first head (or leader of the United States during this end-times period) and four more successive leaders of the broken up regions of the United States from which the Antichrist ultimately takes power before re-unifying three quarters of the United States under his leadership. It is also highly likely that he participates in the tribulation of the church at the fifth seal.

DANIEL'S SEVENTIETH WEEK

It is at the sixth trumpet that Daniel's Seventieth Week begins. Where does this idea of a Seventieth Week come from? What is the significance of a week? To answer that, we have to look at Daniel 9:24-27:

> "Seventy weeks are decreed about your people and your holy city, to finish the transgression, to put an end to sin, and to atone for iniquity, to bring in everlasting righteousness, to seal both vision and prophet, and to anoint a most holy place. Know therefore and understand that from the going out of the word to restore and build Jerusalem to the coming of an anointed one, a prince, there shall be seven weeks. Then for sixty-two weeks it shall be built again with squares and moat, but in a troubled time. And after the sixty-two weeks, an anointed one shall be cut off and shall have nothing. And the people of the prince who is to come shall destroy the city and the sanctuary.

Its end shall come with a flood, and to the end there shall be war. Desolations are decreed. And he shall make a strong covenant with many for one week, and for half of the week he shall put an end to sacrifice and offering. And on the wing of abominations shall come one who makes desolate, until the decreed end is poured out on the desolator."

Verse 24 states that there will be seventy weeks appointed for Israel and Jerusalem. These seventy weeks include:

- Conclusion of Israel's transgression.
- Israel's repentance and atonement.
- Fulfillment of all prophecy and the bringing in of everlasting righteousness.
- Anointing of a most holy place.

It is important to understand what a week represents here. Looking at the period of time beginning with the "taking away" of the burnt offering, we see a span in Revelation 11:2-3 that is equal to three-and-one-half years. This is based on a 360-day year, as is consistent throughout Scripture. The time of Israel's protection in the wilderness (Rev.12:6, 12:14; Dan.7:25, 12:7) is another three-and-one-half years. Adding them together, we have a total of seven years. Knowing from verse 27 that this period is equivalent to one week, we can determine that one week equals seven (360-day) years.

With this information, we can look back in history and find the first sixty-nine weeks (seven weeks [v. 25] + sixty-two weeks [v. 26] or 483 years beginning with the command to rebuild Jerusalem by Artaxerxes [v. 25] in 444 B.C. to Christ's crucifixion (cut off [v. 26] in 28-33 A.D.

Of course, there is much speculation about the exact year of Christ's crucifixion, how we should identify the prince in verse 25, and whether we start with Artaxerxes or Cyrus' decree. Even without knowing the exact timing of the first sixty-nine weeks, however, we know that those weeks end with Christ's crucifixion. Following the cut-off (crucifixion) of the anointed one (Jesus), Jerusalem and the temple are destroyed by "the people of the prince who is to come." The destruction of Jerusalem and the temple in 70 A.D. by the Romans not only identifies the culture from which the prince who is to come (the Antichrist) but also distinguishes this event from the actions of this prince, thereby placing it between the end of the sixty-ninth week and the start of the Seventieth Week. This reveals a gap or pause within this seventy weeks beginning with Israel's rejection of their Messiah and their acceptance of the false prince (Daniel's little horn / Antichrist) as their messiah, triggering the final week, Israel's great tribulation. (See additional comments on this gap in the "Daniel's Fourth Beast: The Beast out of the Sea" section.)

Once we have connected all of these elements, we see how the seals of Revelation fit inside this larger prophetic picture and begin to see many of the characters first described in Daniel emerge onto the world stage. We see the first king of Daniel 8 emerge in the first seal. We see the ten heads (kings) of Daniel 7 arise between the second and third seals. We see the "little horn" (Antichrist) arise prior to the sixth trumpet and probably before the fifth seal.

For a complete summary of the events and personalities of Daniel and how they correlate with the seals, trumpets, and bowls, see chart "The Characters in Daniel."

COMMENTARY ON THE "PROPHECY IN DANIEL" CHART

Prophecy in the book of Daniel focuses on Israel and the nations that have a direct relationship with Israel, either historically or in the future. These nations cover a span of time from the destruction of the world by the Noahatic flood to the destruction of the world by fire at the end of this age.

After the destruction of the temple in 70 A.D. by Rome, the Jews were exiled and dispersed among the nations. As Israel reemerged in 1948 A.D., it found itself in a world dominated by nations that were fragments of the Roman Empire, or the modern West. In the Danielic prophecies, we find this continuation of Roman domination represented as legs changing into feet of iron and clay (Daniel 2) and the terrifying

PROPHECY IN DANIEL
Flood to Fire

Destruction by **FLOOD**

Destruction by **FIRE**

	BABYLON	MEDES / PERSIANS	GREECE	ROME	ROME (Western Civilization)
DAN. 2 Image	Head of Gold — Dan. 2:32, 37-38	Chest of Silver — Dan. 2:32,39	Middle of Bronze — Dan. 2:32,39	Legs of Iron — Dan. 2:33, 40	Feet of Iron and Clay — Dan. 2:33, 41-43; Stone Strikes Image on Feet — Dan. 2:34-35, 44-45
DAN. 7 4 Beasts	Lion — Dan. 7:4	Bear — Dan. 7:5	Leopard — Dan. 7:6	Terrifying, Dreadful, Teeth of Iron, Claws of Bronze — Dan. 7:7,19	Terrifying, Dreadful, Stamps What Is Left With Its Feet (Horns) (Heads) — Dan. 7:7, 19-23; Little Horn Puts Down 3 Horns (Heads) — Dan. 7:20, 24-25; Saints Given into His Hands for Time, Times & Half a Time — Dan. 7:25; Broken by No Human Hand — Dan. 8:25
DAN. 8 Ram & Goat		1st Fulfillment (Figurative): Alexander Defeats Persia — Dan. 8:7,20	Greece Splits Into 4 Nations — Dan. 8:8,22	2nd Fulfillment (Literal): Notable Horn Defeats Persia — Dan. 8:7,20; Little Horn Splits Into 4 Nations — Dan. 8:8,22; Little Horn Rises — Dan. 8:9,23	Regular Burnt Offering Taken Away — Dan. 8:11-12; Destroy Mighty Men — Dan. 8:24; 2,300 Evenings & Mornings Sanct. Restored — Dan. 8:14; He Shall Prosper until Indignation is Accomplished — Dan. 8:25
DAN. 9 70 Weeks		Decree to Rebuild Jerusalem — Ezra 5:13	7 Weeks To an Anointed 62 Weeks Jerusalem Rebuilt — Dan. 9:25	Destruction of City & Sanct. by Anointed People of Ruler One Cut Off To Come — Dan. 9:26	War & Desolations — Dan. 9:26; Covenant for One Week — Dan. 9:27; 1 Week Dan.'s 70th Week Middle of Week End of Sacrifice — Dan. 9:27; Abomination of Desolation — Dan. 9:26; Finish Transgression Seal Up Prophecy — Dan. 9:24
DAN. 11 Kings of North & South		4 Kings — Dan. 11:2	Mighty King — Dan. 11:3; Kingdom Divided Into 4 — Dan. 11:4	Kings of North & South — Dan. 11:5-27; Antiochus Epiphanes; 1st Fulfillment Begins: End Is Yet to Be At The Time Appointed — Dan. 11:27; 2nd Fulfillment Begins: At the Time Appointed — Dan. 11:29	Regular Burnt Offering Taken Away — Dan. 11:31; Abomination Of Desolation — Dan. 11:31; 1st Fulfillment Ends Until The Time of The End For It Still Awaits The Time Appointed — Dan. 11:35; At the Time Of the End — Dan. 11:40; He Shall — Dan. 11:36; Comes To His End — Dan. 11:45
DAN. 12 End Times					Time of Trouble Time, Times & Half a Time — Dan. 12:1, 12:7; Regular Burnt Offering Taken Away — Dan. 12:11; 1,290 Days to Abomination of Desolation — Dan. 12:11; Israel Delivered — Dan. 12:1; 1,335 Days Blessed — Dan. 12:12; Dead Shall Awake — Dan. 12:2

beast of Daniel 7 stamping what was left ("the residue") with its feet. In Daniel 9, we also see this period represented as a pause in prophetic time between the sixty-ninth and the seventieth weeks as Rome destroys the temple (fulfilled in history past) and makes a covenant with Israel (yet to be fulfilled).

It is important to note that in the prophetic sense, the modern West is Rome, the remnants of the old Roman Empire. Using the same methodology implemented to identify Greece in Daniel 8, we can follow the cultural genealogy of the West today directly back to Rome and even further back to Greece. We can, therefore, prophetically identify both Greece and Rome as the modern West. We see this implied by the description of Daniel's fourth beast in Daniel 7:7,19 as having teeth of iron (symbolizing Rome / legs of iron on Nebuchadnezzar's image) and claws of bronze (symbolizing Greece / middle of bronze on Nebuchadnezzar's image).

We also see iron and bronze used symbolically for Rome and Greece in Daniel 4:15, 23 as a band binding the stump representing the continuation of world kingdoms following the cutting down of the tree representing Babylon. This tree is the world's economic substitute for the tree of life we no longer have access to since the fall (Gen. 2:22-24) but will once again in the new Heaven and New Earth (Rev. 22:2). It also can be viewed as a substitute for the Kingdom of Heaven Jesus described in the parable of the mustard seed (Matt. 13:31-32 / Mark 4:30-32). The symbolism of the stump as a lessor form of the original tree is also used to describe the remnant of Israel entering into the millennial Kingdom of our Lord (Isaiah 6:13). Together, these descriptions show the continuation of Western culture in the beast of Revelation and how they are a substitute for God's provision.

As this chart suggests, the political institutions of the world have their beginnings in Babylon following the flood. It is also in Babylon that we find the origins of the false religions of the world, thus our ability to identify "Babylon the great" as the woman in Revelation 17.

THE DAY OF THE LORD

The day of the Lord is a distinct period of time described throughout Scripture. This period begins at the blowing of the seventh trumpet when the angel declares, "The kingdoms of the world become the kingdom of our Lord." Just as that statement suggests, the day of the Lord is the process of God taking back control of his creation, beginning with his removal of evil from heaven by throwing down Satan and those angels who followed him. At the same time, Christ removes his elect from the earth (the rapture) in preparation for removing evil from the earth by pouring out his unrestrained wrath in the bowl judgments. At Christ's second coming, this process pauses as Christ reigns peacefully for one thousand years, shifting history from a time of darkness (withdrawal of his presence as creation's order breaks down) to light (his presence). His wrath then briefly resumes at the end of the thousand years with the final removal of Satan and the judgment of the lost, who are thrown into the lake of fire. This completes the day of the Lord and ushers in the new heaven and earth.

To see the events that characterize this period of time more clearly, let's look at some of the scriptural passages that describe the day of the Lord in great detail.

Isaiah 13:6-16

"Wail, for the day of the Lord is near;
as destruction from the Almighty it will come!

Therefore all hands will be feeble,
  and every human heart will melt.
They will be dismayed:
    pangs and agony will seize them;
    they will be in anguish like a woman in labor.
They will look aghast at one another;
    their faces will be aflame.
Behold, the day of the Lord comes,
    cruel, with wrath and fierce anger,
to make the land a desolation
    and to destroy its sinners from it.
For the stars of the heavens and their constellations
    will not give their light;
the sun will be dark at its rising,
    and the moon will not shed its light.

I will punish the world for its evil,
    and the wicked for their iniquity;
I will put an end to the pomp of the arrogant,
     and lay low the pompous pride of the ruthless.
I will make people more rare than fine gold,
    and mankind than the gold of Ophir.

Therefore I will make the heavens tremble,
    and the earth will be shaken out of its place,
at the wrath of the Lord of hosts
    in the day of his fierce anger.
And like a hunted gazelle,
    or like sheep with none to gather them,
each will turn to his own people,
    and each will flee to his own land.

Whoever is found will be thrust through,
    and whoever is caught will fall by the sword.
Their infants will be dashed in pieces
    before their eyes;

their houses will be plundered
and their wives ravished."

Joel 2

"Blow a trumpet in Zion;
sound an alarm on my holy mountain!
Let all the inhabitants of the land tremble,
for the day of the Lord is coming; it is near,
a day of darkness and gloom,
a day of clouds and thick darkness!
Like blackness there is spread upon the mountains
a great and powerful people;
their like has never been before,
nor will be again after them
through the years of all generations.

Fire devours before them,
and behind them a flame burns.
The land is like the garden of Eden before them,
but behind them a desolate wilderness,
and nothing escapes them.
Their appearance is like the appearance of horses,
and like war horses they run.
As with the rumbling of chariots,
they leap on the tops of the mountains,
like the crackling of a flame of fire
devouring the stubble,
like a powerful army
drawn up for battle.

Before them peoples are in anguish;
all faces grow pale.
Like warriors they charge;
like soldiers they scale the wall.
They march each on his way;
they do not swerve from their paths.

They do not jostle one another;
 each marches in his path;
they burst through the weapons
 and are not halted.
They leap upon the city,
 they run upon the walls,
they climb up into the houses,
  they enter through the windows like a thief.

The earth quakes before them;
 the heavens tremble.
The sun and the moon are darkened,
 and the stars withdraw their shining.
The Lord utters his voice
 before his army,
for his camp is exceedingly great;
 he who executes his word is powerful.
For the day of the Lord is great and very awesome;
 who can endure it?

'Yet even now,' declares the Lord,
 'return to me with all your heart,
with fasting, with weeping, and with mourning;
 and rend your hearts and not your garments.'
Return to the Lord your God,
 for he is gracious and merciful,
slow to anger, and abounding in steadfast love;
 and he relents over disaster.
Who knows whether he will not turn and relent,
 and leave a blessing behind him,
a grain offering and a drink offering
 for the Lord your God?

Blow the trumpet in Zion;
 consecrate a fast;

call a solemn assembly;
   gather the people.
Consecrate the congregation;
   assemble the elders;
gather the children,
   even nursing infants.
Let the bridegroom leave his room,
   and the bride her chamber.

Between the vestibule and the altar
   let the priests, the ministers of the Lord, weep
and say, 'Spare your people, O Lord,
   and make not your heritage a reproach,
   a byword among the nations.
Why should they say among the peoples,
   "Where is their God?"'"

This passage not only describes the destruction of the day of the Lord but also the joy that will come at its conclusion when Christ reigns over the nations during the millennium. At this point, the passage begins to describe this peaceful period, which follows God's judgment.

"Then the Lord became jealous for his land
   and had pity on his people.
The Lord answered and said to his people,
'Behold, I am sending to you
   grain, wine, and oil,
   and you will be satisfied;
and I will no more make you
   a reproach among the nations.

'I will remove the northerner far from you,
   and drive him into a parched and desolate land,
his vanguard into the eastern sea,
   and his rear guard into the western sea;
the stench and foul smell of him will rise,
   for he has done great things.

'Fear not, O land;
    be glad and rejoice,
    for the Lord has done great things!
Fear not, you beasts of the field,
    for the pastures of the wilderness are green;
the tree bears its fruit;
    the fig tree and vine give their full yield.

'Be glad, O children of Zion,
    and rejoice in the Lord your God,
for he has given the early rain for your vindication;
    he has poured down for you abundant rain,
    the early and the latter rain, as before.

'The threshing floors shall be full of grain;
    the vats shall overflow with wine and oil.
I will restore to you the years
    that the swarming locust has eaten,
the hopper, the destroyer, and the cutter,
    my great army, which I sent among you.

'You shall eat in plenty and be satisfied,
    and praise the name of the Lord your God,
    who has dealt wondrously with you.
And my people shall never again be put to shame.
You shall know that I am in the midst of Israel,
    and that I am the Lord your God and there is none else.
And my people shall never again be put to shame.

'And it shall come to pass afterward,
    that I will pour out my Spirit on all flesh;
your sons and your daughters shall prophesy,
    your old men shall dream dreams,
    and your young men shall see visions.
Even on the male and female servants
    in those days I will pour out my Spirit.

'And I will show wonders in the heavens and on the earth, blood and fire and columns of smoke. The sun shall be turned to darkness, and the moon to blood, before the great and awesome day of the Lord comes. And it shall come to pass that everyone who calls on the name of the Lord shall be saved. For in Mount Zion and in Jerusalem there shall be those who escape, as the Lord has said, and among the survivors shall be those whom the Lord calls.'"

Joel 3

"For behold, in those days and at that time, when I restore the fortunes of Judah and Jerusalem, I will gather all the nations and bring them down to the Valley of Jehoshaphat. And I will enter into judgment with them there, on behalf of my people and my heritage Israel, because they have scattered them among the nations and have divided up my land, and have cast lots for my people, and have traded a boy for a prostitute, and have sold a girl for wine and have drunk it.

'What are you to me, O Tyre and Sidon, and all the regions of Philistia? Are you paying me back for something? If you are paying me back, I will return your payment on your own head swiftly and speedily. For you have taken my silver and my gold, and have carried my rich treasures into your temples. You have sold the people of Judah and Jerusalem to the Greeks in order to remove them far from their own border. Behold, I will stir them up from the place to which you have sold them, and I will return your payment on your own head. I will sell your sons and your daughters into the hand of the people of Judah, and they will sell them to the Sabeans, to a nation far away, for the Lord has spoken.'

Proclaim this among the nations:
Consecrate for war;
   stir up the mighty men.
Let all the men of war draw near;
   let them come up.
Beat your plowshares into swords,

and your pruning hooks into spears;
let the weak say, 'I am a warrior.'

Hasten and come,
all you surrounding nations,
and gather yourselves there.
Bring down your warriors, O Lord.
Let the nations stir themselves up
and come up to the Valley of Jehoshaphat;
for there I will sit to judge
all the surrounding nations.

Put in the sickle,
for the harvest is ripe.
Go in, tread,
for the winepress is full.
The vats overflow,
for their evil is great.

Multitudes, multitudes,
in the valley of decision!
For the day of the Lord is near
in the valley of decision.
The sun and the moon are darkened,
and the stars withdraw their shining.

The Lord roars from Zion,
and utters his voice from Jerusalem,
and the heavens and the earth quake.
But the Lord is a refuge to his people,
a stronghold to the people of Israel.

'So you shall know that I am the Lord your God,
who dwells in Zion, my holy mountain.
And Jerusalem shall be holy,
and strangers shall never again pass through it.

'And in that day
the mountains shall drip sweet wine,
and the hills shall flow with milk,
and all the streambeds of Judah
shall flow with water;
and a fountain shall come forth from the house of the Lord
and water the Valley of Shittim.

'Egypt shall become a desolation
and Edom a desolate wilderness,
for the violence done to the people of Judah,
because they have shed innocent blood in their land.
But Judah shall be inhabited forever,
and Jerusalem to all generations.
I will avenge their blood,
blood I have not avenged,
for the Lord dwells in Zion.'"

Obadiah 1:15-21

"For the day of the Lord is near upon all the nations.
As you have done, it shall be done to you;
your deeds shall return on your own head.
For as you have drunk on my holy mountain,
so all the nations shall drink continually;
they shall drink and swallow,
and shall be as though they had never been.
But in Mount Zion there shall be those who escape,
and it shall be holy,
and the house of Jacob shall possess their own possessions.
The house of Jacob shall be a fire,
and the house of Joseph a flame,
and the house of Esau stubble;
they shall burn them and consume them,
and there shall be no survivor for the house of Esau,
for the Lord has spoken.

Those of the Negeb shall possess Mount Esau,
    and those of the Shephelah shall possess the land of the Philistines;
they shall possess the land of Ephraim and the land of Samaria,
    and Benjamin shall possess Gilead.
The exiles of this host of the people of Israel
    shall possess the land of the Canaanites as far as Zarephath,
and the exiles of Jerusalem who are in Sepharad
    shall possess the cities of the Negeb.
Saviors shall go up to Mount Zion
    to rule Mount Esau,
    and the kingdom shall be the Lord's."

Zephaniah 1

"The word of the Lord that came to Zephaniah the son of Cushi, son of Gedaliah, son of Amariah, son of Hezekiah, in the days of Josiah the son of Amon, king of Judah.

'I will utterly sweep away everything
    from the face of the earth,' declares the Lord.
'I will sweep away man and beast;
    I will sweep away the birds of the heavens
    and the fish of the sea,
and the rubble with the wicked.
    I will cut off mankind
    from the face of the earth,' declares the Lord.
'I will stretch out my hand against Judah
    and against all the inhabitants of Jerusalem;
and I will cut off from this place the remnant of Baal
    and the name of the idolatrous priests along with the priests,
those who bow down on the roofs
    to the host of the heavens,
those who bow down and swear to the Lord
    and yet swear by Milcom,
those who have turned back from following the Lord,
    who do not seek the Lord or inquire of him.'

Be silent before the Lord God!
  For the day of the Lord is near;
the Lord has prepared a sacrifice
  and consecrated his guests.
And on the day of the Lord's sacrifice—
'I will punish the officials and the king's sons
  and all who array themselves in foreign attire.
On that day I will punish
  everyone who leaps over the threshold,
and those who fill their master's house
  with violence and fraud.

'On that day,' declares the Lord,
  'a cry will be heard from the Fish Gate,
a wail from the Second Quarter,
  a loud crash from the hills.
Wail, O inhabitants of the Mortar!
  For all the traders are no more;
  all who weigh out silver are cut off.
At that time I will search Jerusalem with lamps,
  and I will punish the men
who are complacent,
    those who say in their hearts,
'The Lord will not do good,
  nor will he do ill.'
Their goods shall be plundered,
  and their houses laid waste.
Though they build houses,
  they shall not inhabit them;
though they plant vineyards,
  they shall not drink wine from them.'

The great day of the Lord is near,
  near and hastening fast;
the sound of the day of the Lord is bitter;
    the mighty man cries aloud there.

A day of wrath is that day,
    a day of distress and anguish,
a day of ruin and devastation,
    a day of darkness and gloom,
a day of clouds and thick darkness,
    a day of trumpet blast and battle cry
against the fortified cities
    and against the lofty battlements.

I will bring distress on mankind,
    so that they shall walk like the blind,
    because they have sinned against the Lord;
their blood shall be poured out like dust,
    and their flesh like dung.
Neither their silver nor their gold
    shall be able to deliver them
    on the day of the wrath of the Lord.
In the fire of his jealousy,
    all the earth shall be consumed;
for a full and sudden end
    he will make of all the inhabitants of the earth."

Zechariah 14

"Behold, a day is coming for the Lord, when the spoil taken from you will be divided in your midst. For I will gather all the nations against Jerusalem to battle, and the city shall be taken and the houses plundered and the women raped. Half of the city shall go out into exile, but the rest of the people shall not be cut off from the city. Then the Lord will go out and fight against those nations as when he fights on a day of battle. On that day his feet shall stand on the Mount of Olives that lies before Jerusalem on the east, and the Mount of Olives shall be split in two from east to west by a very wide valley, so that one half of the Mount shall move northward, and the other half southward. And you shall flee to the valley of my mountains, for the valley of the mountains shall reach to Azal. And you shall flee as you fled from the earthquake in the days of Uzziah king of Judah. Then the Lord my God will come, and all the holy ones with him.

On that day there shall be no light, cold, or frost. And there shall be a unique day, which is known to the Lord, neither day nor night, but at evening time there shall be light.

On that day living waters shall flow out from Jerusalem, half of them to the eastern sea and half of them to the western sea. It shall continue in summer as in winter.

And the Lord will be king over all the earth. On that day the Lord will be one and his name one.

The whole land shall be turned into a plain from Geba to Rimmon south of Jerusalem. But Jerusalem shall remain aloft on its site from the Gate of Benjamin to the place of the former gate, to the Corner Gate, and from the Tower of Hananel to the king's winepresses. And it shall be inhabited, for there shall never again be a decree of utter destruction. Jerusalem shall dwell in security.

And this shall be the plague with which the Lord will strike all the peoples that wage war against Jerusalem: their flesh will rot while they are still standing on their feet, their eyes will rot in their sockets, and their tongues will rot in their mouths.

And on that day a great panic from the Lord shall fall on them, so that each will seize the hand of another, and the hand of the one will be raised against the hand of the other. Even Judah will fight at Jerusalem. And the wealth of all the surrounding nations shall be collected, gold, silver, and garments in great abundance. And a plague like this plague shall fall on the horses, the mules, the camels, the donkeys, and whatever beasts may be in those camps.

Then everyone who survives of all the nations that have come against Jerusalem shall go up year after year to worship the King, the Lord of hosts, and to keep the Feast of Booths. And if any of the families of the earth do not go up to Jerusalem to worship the King, the Lord of hosts, there will be no rain on them. And if the family of Egypt does not go up and present themselves, then on them there shall be no rain; there shall be the plague with which the Lord afflicts the nations that do not go up to keep the Feast of Booths. This shall be the punishment to Egypt and the punishment to all the nations that do not go up to keep the Feast of Booths.

And on that day there shall be inscribed on the bells of the horses, 'Holy to the Lord.' And the pots in the house of the Lord shall be as the bowls before the altar. And every pot in Jerusalem and Judah shall be holy to the Lord of hosts, so that all who sacrifice may come and take of them and boil the meat of the sacrifice in them. And there shall no longer be a trader in the house of the Lord of hosts on that day."

Malachi 4

"For behold, the day is coming, burning like an oven, when all the arrogant and all evildoers will be stubble. The day that is coming shall set them ablaze, says the Lord of hosts, so that it will leave them neither root nor branch. But for you who fear my name, the sun of righteousness shall rise with healing in its wings. You shall go out leaping like calves from the stall. And you shall tread down the wicked, for they will be ashes under the soles of your feet, on the day when I act, says the Lord of hosts.

"Remember the law of my servant Moses, the statutes and rules that I commanded him at Horeb for all Israel.

"Behold, I will send you Elijah the prophet before the great and awesome day of the Lord comes. And he will turn the hearts of fathers to their children and the hearts of children to their fathers, lest I come and strike the land with a decree of utter destruction."

The Day of the Lord is described in the New Testament, as well. In these passages, the writers build on the teaching of the Old Testament prophets and add detail. In many cases, this detail involves the Antichrist and his role during this time.

1 Thessalonians 5:1-10

"Now concerning the times and the seasons, brothers, you have no need to have anything written to you. For you yourselves are fully aware that the day of the Lord will come like a thief in the night. While people are saying, 'There is peace and security,' then sudden destruction will come upon them as labor pains come upon a pregnant woman, and they will not escape. But you are not in darkness, brothers, for that day to surprise you like a thief. For you are all children of light, children of the day. We are not of the night or of the darkness. So then let us not sleep, as others do, but let us keep awake and be sober. For those who sleep, sleep at night, and those who get drunk, are drunk at night. But since we belong to the day, let us be sober, having put on the breastplate of faith and love, and for a helmet the hope of salvation. For God has not destined us for wrath, but to obtain salvation through our Lord Jesus Christ, who died for us so that whether we are awake or asleep we might live with him."

2 Thessalonians 2:1-12

"Now concerning the coming of our Lord Jesus Christ and our being gathered together to him, we ask you, brothers, not to be quickly shaken in mind or alarmed, either by a spirit or a spoken word, or a letter seeming to be from us, to the effect that the day of the Lord has come. Let no one deceive you in any way. For that day will not come, unless the rebellion comes first, and the man of lawlessness is revealed, the son of destruction, who opposes and exalts himself against every so-called god or object of worship, so that he takes his seat in the temple of God, proclaiming himself to be God. Do you not remember that when I was still with you I told you these things? And you know what is restraining him now so that he may be revealed in his time. For the mystery of lawlessness is already at work. Only he who now restrains it will do so until he is out of the way. And then the lawless one will be revealed, whom the Lord Jesus will kill with the breath of his mouth and bring to nothing by the appearance of his coming. The coming of the lawless one is by the activity of Satan with all power and false signs and wonders, and with all wicked deception for those who are perishing, because they refused to love the truth and so be saved. Therefore God sends them a strong delusion, so that they may believe what is false, in order that all may be condemned who did not believe the truth but had pleasure in unrighteousness."

2 Peter 3:1-13

"This is now the second letter that I am writing to you, beloved. In both of them I am stirring up your sincere mind by way of reminder, that you should remember the predictions of the holy prophets and the commandment of the Lord and Savior through your apostles, knowing this first of all, that scoffers will come in the last days with scoffing, following their own sinful desires. They will say, 'Where is the promise of his coming? For ever since the fathers fell asleep, all things are continuing as they were from the beginning of creation.'

For they deliberately overlook this fact, that the heavens existed long ago, and the earth was formed out of water and through water by the word of God, and that by means of these the world that then existed was deluged with water and perished. But by the same word the heavens and earth that now exist are stored up for fire, being kept until the day of judgment and destruction of the ungodly.

But do not overlook this one fact, beloved, that with the Lord one day is as a thousand years, and a thousand years as one day. The Lord is not slow to fulfill his promise as some count slowness, but is patient toward you, not wishing that any should perish, but that all should reach repentance. But the day of the Lord will come like a thief, and then the heavens will pass away with a roar, and the heavenly bodies will be burned up and dissolved, and the earth and the works that are done on it will be exposed.

Since all these things are thus to be dissolved, what sort of people ought you to be in lives of holiness and godliness, waiting for and hastening the coming of the day of God, because of which the heavens will be set on fire and dissolved, and the heavenly bodies will melt as they burn! But according to his promise we are waiting for new heavens and a new earth in which righteousness dwells."

THE FEASTS OF
THE LORD

In Revelation, the focus is initially on the body of Christ, the church, but once the church is either martyred or raptured, God turns his focus back to Israel. This occurs at the harvest of the earth in Revelation 14. Thus it should be no surprise that, from this point on, we begin to see symbolism that ties in with the nation's historic feasts. Therefore, in order to understand how and why the events of Revelation unfold as they do, it's helpful to back up and define these feasts so that the symbolism becomes clear.

There are seven feasts that God set down for Israel, not including the weekly Sabbath (Leviticus 23). These feasts represent the character and nature of God, man's relationship to God, and at the time they were set down, foreshadowed events that were to occur in the future (Col. 2:16-17). There are four spring feasts (Firstfruits, Unleavened Bread, Passover, and Pentecost) and three fall feasts (Trumpets, Atonement, and Tabernacles). First we will look at the spring feasts.

The spring feasts take place in the month of Nisan, which corresponds to the month of April in the Gregorian calendar.

Passover (Pesach) is a reminder of how, while living in Egypt, the Angel of Death spared (passed over) the homes of the people of Israel. In the tenth plague sent against Egypt, God warned that the Angel of Death would pass by the homes of all who dwelt in Egypt and take their firstborn sons. But he also promised that if the people of Israel would spread the blood of a sacrificial lamb over their doorways, their sons would be spared. That night, the Angel of Death passed by as prophesied, and as such, the firstborn sons of the Egyptians died. But also as promised, when the Angel of Death saw the blood spread over the lintels of the Israelites, their firstborn sons were spared. This pointed to our protection and eternal preservation through the sacrificial blood of the Christ, the perfect Lamb of God. On the cross, Jesus shed his blood as an atonement for our sin and thereby fulfilled the Feast of Passover that the Israelites began rehearsing in the days of Moses after the Exodus. The fulfillment of this feast occurred on Passover at the precise time the priests were sacrificing the Passover Lamb.

Unleavened Bread is a reminder of the hasty departure of Israel from Egypt, in which the Israelites wrapped their unleavened bread in cloths for the journey, when Moses led them out of bondage to the Pharaoh. Ultimately, this feast foreshadows the death (departure) and burial (wrapping in burial cloth) of Christ, who leads us out of the bondage of sin.

Firstfruits is a reminder of God's provision, the first of the spring harvest. In this feast, Israel waves a sheaf of grain before the Lord as an offering (sacrifice) back to God. It was to be offered the day after the weekly Sabbath during the week of the Feast of Unleavened Bread. This coincided with the first day of the week when Mary first saw Jesus following his resurrection and was told not to touch him until he ascended to the Father (John 20:17). Jesus subsequently ascended (offered himself up) to the Father prior to appearing to Thomas eight days later (John 20:27) and completed the requirements of the Feast of Firstfruits discussed by Paul in 1 Corinthians 15:20-23.

Pentecost (Shavuot / Weeks) takes place in the month of Sivan (corresponding to the month of May–June in the Gregorian calendar). It is a reminder of the delivering of the law to Israel at Mount Sinai and occurs seven weeks following the day after Feast of Firstfruits (fifty days). We find fulfillment of this feast in the delivering of the Holy Spirit to the one hundred and twenty (Acts 2:1-3), thereby writing the law on their hearts (Rom. 2:15).

These spring feasts were prophetic of Christ's first coming. Next we will look at the fall feasts, which are prophetic of his second coming.

Trumpets (Rosh Hashanah) is celebrated on the first two days of Tishrei, corresponding to the months of September–October. This was "a day of blowing" of the shofar, calling the people to prepare for God's judgment as well as to the civil new year. It foreshadows the ultimate vindication of the righteous and the judgment of the wicked by God. For Israel, it points directly to the day in which Israel begins her national repentance and subsequent introspection leading to her atonement. For the church, it points to the day that she goes before the judgment seat of Christ (2 Cor. 5:10).

The Feast of Trumpets is the first of the fall feasts to be fulfilled and occurs at the harvest of the earth. At this time, Jesus appears in the sky, not as the Suffering Servant but as the Lion of the Tribe of Judah. He comes to conduct two reapings: the reaping of the elect, which includes both the harvesting of the church at the rapture, (1 Thess. 4:16-17) and the atonement of national Israel.

Day of Atonement (Yom Kippur) occurs during the month of Tishrei. For the nation of Israel, it was the holiest and most solemn day of the year. Between the Feast of Trumpets and the Day of Atonement are ten days - the Days of Awe - a time of national reflection and repentance leading to the nation's day of atonement. Ultimately, this feast points to the day for which national Israel's rejection of Jesus is atoned and the remnant of Israel is restored.

Tabernacles (Sukkot / Booths) also occurs during the month of Tishrei. It is a reminder of Israel's forty years of living in tents while in the wilderness of Sinai. This, and ultimately all of these feasts, will lead to the fulfillment of the Feast of Tabernacles in the one-thousand-year reign of Christ when Christ tabernacles (dwells) with us.

Understanding the fall feasts not only reinforces the chronology found in Revelation but also speaks volumes on the depth and precision of God's plan. He has had Israel rehearsing these feasts for thousands of years, not only as a commemoration of his past faithfulness but also of his future faithfulness to the reconciliation of Israel to himself at the time of the end.

We also see God using the redemption of the Gentiles at the Feast of Trumpets to provoke jealousy in Israel even as Paul foresaw their salvation:

"So I ask, did they stumble in order that they might fall? By no means! Rather through their trespass salvation has come to the Gentiles, so as to make Israel jealous. Now if their trespass means riches for the world, and if their failure means riches for the Gentiles, how much more will their full inclusion mean!" (Rom. 11:11-12).

Through the fulfillment of the fall feasts, we also see how when the natural branches (all of Israel) are grafted back in, the fullness of the Scriptures in Christ will be fully realized:

"But if some of the branches were broken off, and you, although a wild olive shoot, were grafted in among the others and now share in the nourishing root of the olive tree, do not be arrogant toward the branches. If you are, remember it is not you who support the root, but the root that supports you. Then you will say, 'Branches were broken off so that I might be grafted in.' That is true. They were broken off because of their unbelief, but you stand fast through faith. So do not become proud, but fear. For if God did not spare the natural branches, neither will he spare you. Note then the kindness and the severity of God: severity toward those who have fallen, but God's kindness to you, provided you continue in his kindness. Otherwise you too will be cut off. And even they, if they do not continue in their unbelief, will be grafted in, for God has the power to graft them in again. For if you were cut from what is by nature a wild olive tree, and grafted, contrary to nature, into a cultivated olive tree, how much more will these, the natural branches, be grafted back into their own olive tree" (Rom. 11: 17-24).

Below is a table illustrating the relationships between the feasts, the events ultimately foreshadowed by the feasts, and where they are fulfilled in Revelation:

Feast	Event	Revelation Fulfillment
Trumpets	**Rapture** Matt. 24:30-31 Mark 13:26-27 Luke 21:27-28 1 Cor. 15:51-52 1 Thess. 4:16-17	**Harvest of the Earth** Rev. 14:14-16
Yom Kippur	**Israel's Atonement** Is. 25:9 Is. 27:12-13 Jer. 31:31-40 Jer. 33:14-26 Ezek. 36:25-27 Ezek. 37:23 Hos. 3:4-5 Hos. 6:1-3 Joel 2:17-32 Zech. 3:8-10 Zech. 12:7-14 Zech. 13:1-9	**Harvest of the Earth** **(10 Days Following** **the Feast of Trumpets)** Rev. 14:14-16
Tabernacles	**1000 Yr. Reign of Christ** Is. 11:1-10 Ezek. 36:28-36 Ezek. 37:24-28 Ezek. 39:25-29 Ezek. 40-48 Amos 9:11-15 Zeph. 3:9-20 Zech. 8:1-17	**Jesus' Second Coming** **to the Great White** **Throne Judgment** Rev. 19:11 to Rev. 20:11

THE CHRONOLOGICAL OVERLAY OF PROPHECY IN THE SYNOPTIC GOSPELS
ON THE BOOK OF REVELATION

This appendix has been created in an effort to illustrate how the chronology of prophetic passages in the synoptic gospels is maintained as they are overlaid onto the book of Revelation. Key verses have been listed in chronological order, along with their corresponding verses from Revelation. What is revealed is God's intentional chronological organization of prophecy given by Jesus to his disciples as documented by Matthew, Mark, and Luke, and John in Revelation.

The most profound evidence of this chronological parallel is found in Matthew 24 and 25, where we see a complete description of the time of the end beginning with Revelation's first seal and ending with God's final judgment.

The Chronological Overlay of
MATTHEW ON REVELATION

First in our series of overlays are the end-times passages in the gospel of Matthew. The overlay with Revelation begins with Matthew 24:5 and continues uninterrupted through verse 31. Beginning in verse 32, Jesus interrupts his discussion of the signs of his coming and the end of the age with general statements of timing and an admonition to remain prepared. He then continues this discussion in Matthew 25:1 using two parables to explain in greater detail the nature of his coming in the clouds (rapture) as described in Matthew 24:30-31. The parable of the ten virgins (Matt. 25:1-13) illustrates how the elect are removed and Israel is left behind just prior to the nation's repentance. The parable of the ten talents (Matt. 25:14-30) alludes to the purification process of the elect on the sea of glass and fire. The discussion of the end of the age then resumes with a description of the final judgment beginning in Matthew 25:31-46.

Beginnings of Birth Pains

Matthew 24:5

"For many will come in my name, saying I am the Christ, and they will lead many astray."

Revelation 6:1-2

"Now I watched when the Lamb opened one of the seven seals, and I heard one of the four living creatures say with a voice like thunder, 'Come!' And I looked, and behold, a white horse! And its rider had a bow, and a crown was given to him, and he came out conquering, and to conquer."

Matthew 24:6-7

"And you will hear of wars and rumors of war. See that you are not alarmed, for this must take place, but the end is not yet. For nation will rise against nation, and kingdom against kingdom."

Revelation 6:3-4

"When he opened the second seal, I heard the second living creature say, 'Come!' And out came another horse, bright red. Its rider was permitted to take peace from the earth."

Matthew 24:7-8

"And there will be famines and earthquakes in various places. All these are but the beginnings of birth pains."

Revelation 6:7-8

"When he opened the fourth seal, I heard the voice of the fourth living creature say, 'Come!' And I looked, and behold, a pale horse! And its rider's name was Death, and Hades followed him. And they were given authority over a fourth of the earth, to kill with sword and with famine and with pestilence and by wild beasts of the earth."

Great Tribulation of the Church

Matthew 24:9-14

"Then they will deliver you up to tribulation and put you to death, and you will be hated by all nations for my name's sake. And then many will fall away and betray one another and hate one another. And many false prophets will arise and lead many astray. And because lawlessness will be increased, the love of many will grow cold. But the one who endures to the end will be saved. And this gospel of the kingdom will be proclaimed throughout the whole world as a testimony to all nations, and then the end will come."

Revelation 6:9-11, 7:9-17

"When he opened the fifth seal, I saw under the altar the souls of those who had been slain for the word of God and for the witness they had borne. They cried out with a loud voice, 'O Sovereign Lord, holy and true, how long before you will judge and avenge our blood on those who dwell on the earth?' Then they were each given a white robe and told to rest a little longer, until the number of their fellow servants and their brothers should be complete, who were to be killed as they themselves had been…

After this I looked, and behold, a great multitude that no one could number, from every nation, from all tribes and peoples and languages, standing before the throne and before the Lamb, clothed in white robes, with palm branches in their hands, and crying out with a loud voice, 'Salvation belongs to our God who sits on the throne, and to the Lamb!' And all the angels were standing around the throne and around the elders and the four living creatures, and they fell on their faces before the throne and worshiped God, saying, 'Amen! Blessing and glory and wisdom and thanksgiving and honor and power and might be to our God forever and ever! Amen.'

Then one of the elders addressed me, saying, 'Who are these, clothed in white robes, and from where have they come?' I said to him, 'Sir, you know.' And he said to me, 'These are the ones coming out of the great tribulation. They have washed their robes and made them white in the blood of the Lamb.

'Therefore they are before the throne of God,
    and serve him day and night in his temple; and he who
    sits on the throne will shelter them with his presence.
They shall hunger no more, neither thirst anymore;
    the sun shall not strike them, nor any scorching heat.
For the Lamb in the midst of the throne will be their shepherd,
    and he will guide them to springs of living water,
    and God will wipe away every tear from their eyes.'"

Great Tribulation of Israel

Matthew 24:15-22

"So when you see the abomination of desolation spoken of by the prophet Daniel, standing in the holy place (let the reader understand), then let those who are in Judea flee to the mountains. Let the one who is on the housetop not go down to take what is in his house, and let the one who is in the field not turn back to take his cloak. And alas for women who are pregnant and for those who are nursing infants in those days! Pray that your flight may not be in winter or on a Sabbath. For then there will be great tribulation, such as has not been from the beginning of the world until now, no, and never will be. And if those days had not been cut short, no human being would be saved. But for the sake of the elect those days will be cut short."

Revelation 12:6; 13-16

"And the woman fled into the wilderness, where she has a place prepared by God, in which she is to be nourished for 1,260 days...

And when the dragon saw that he had been thrown down to the earth, he pursued the woman who had given birth to the male child. But the woman was given the two wings of the great eagle so that she might fly from the serpent into the wilderness, to the place where she is to be nourished for a time, and times, and half a time. The serpent poured water like a river out of his mouth after the woman, to sweep her away with a flood. But the earth came to the help of the woman, and the earth opened its mouth and swallowed the river that the dragon had poured from his mouth."

Heavenly Powers Shaken, Stars / Angels Fall

Matthew 24:29

"Immediately after the tribulation of those days the sun will be darkened, and the moon will not give its light, and the stars will fall from heaven, and the powers of the heavens will be shaken."

Revelation 12:7-11

"Now war arose in heaven, Michael and his angels fighting against the dragon. And the dragon and his angels fought back, but he was defeated, and there was no longer any place for them in heaven. And the great dragon was thrown down, that ancient serpent, who is called the devil and Satan, the deceiver of the whole world—he was thrown down to the earth, and his angels were thrown down with him. And I heard a loud voice in heaven, saying, 'Now the salvation and the power and the kingdom of our God and the authority of his Christ have come, for the accuser of our brothers has been thrown down, who accuses them day and night before our God. And they have conquered him by the blood of the Lamb and by the word of their testimony, for they loved not their lives even unto death.'"

Son of Man in the Clouds Gathering / Harvesting His Elect

Matthew 24:30-31

"Then will appear in heaven, the sign of the Son of Man, and then all the tribes of the earth will mourn, and they will see the *Son of Man coming on the clouds* of heaven with power and great glory. And he will send out his Angels with a loud trumpet call, and they *will gather His elect* from the four winds, from one end of heaven to the other." *(emphasis mine)*

Revelation 14:14-16

"Then I looked, and behold, a white cloud, and *seated on the cloud one like a son of man*, with a golden crown on his head, and a sharp sickle in his hand. And another angel came out of the temple, calling with a loud voice to him who sat on the cloud, '*Put in your sickle, and reap*, for the hour to reap has come, for the harvest of the earth is fully ripe.' So he who sat on the cloud swung his sickle across the earth, and the earth was reaped." *(emphasis mine)*

Second Coming of Jesus and Final Judgment

Matthew 25:31-46

"When the Son of Man comes in his glory, and all the angels with him, then he will sit on his glorious throne. Before him will be gathered all the nations, and he will separate people one from another as a shepherd separates the sheep from the goats. And he will place the sheep on his right, but the goats on the left. Then the King will say to those on his right, 'Come, you who are blessed by my Father, inherit the kingdom prepared for you from the foundation of the world. For I was hungry and you gave me food, I was thirsty and you gave me drink, I was a stranger and you welcomed me, I was naked and you clothed me, I was sick and you visited me, I was in prison and you came to me.' Then the righteous will answer him, saying, 'Lord, when did we see you hungry and feed you, or thirsty and give you drink? And when did we see you a stranger and welcome you, or naked and clothe you? And when did we see you sick or in prison and visit you?' And the King will answer them, 'Truly, I say to you, as you did it to one of the least of these my brothers, you did it to me.' Then he will say to those on his left, 'Depart from me, you cursed, into the eternal fire prepared for the devil and his angels. For I was hungry and you gave me no food, I was thirsty and you gave me no drink, I was a stranger and you did not welcome me, naked and you did not clothe me, sick and in prison and you did not visit me.' Then they also will answer, saying, 'Lord, when did we see you hungry or thirsty or a stranger or naked or sick or in prison, and did not minister to you?' Then he will answer them, saying, 'Truly, I say to you, as you did not do it to one of the least of these, you did not do it to me.' And these will go away into eternal punishment, but the righteous into eternal life."

Revelation 19:11-16; 20:11-15

"Then I saw heaven opened, and behold, a white horse! The one sitting on it is called Faithful and True, and in righteousness he judges and makes war. His eyes are like a flame of fire, and on his head are many diadems, and he has a name written that no one knows but himself. He is clothed in a robe dipped in blood, and the name by which he is called is The Word of God. And the armies of heaven, arrayed in fine linen, white and pure, were following him on white horses. From his mouth comes a sharp sword with which to strike down the nations, and he will rule them with a rod of iron. He will tread the winepress of the fury of the wrath of God the Almighty. On his robe and on his thigh he has a name written, King of kings and Lord of lords...

Then I saw a great white throne and him who was seated on it. From his presence earth and sky fled away, and no place was found for them. And I saw the dead, great and small, standing before the throne, and books were opened. Then another book was opened, which is the book of life. And the dead were judged by what was written in the books, according to what they had done. And the sea gave up the dead who were in it, Death and Hades gave up the dead who were in them, and they were judged, each one of them, according to what they had done. Then Death and Hades were thrown into the lake of fire. This is the second death, the lake of fire. And if anyone's name was not found written in the book of life, he was thrown into the lake of fire."

The Chronological Overlay of
MARK ON REVELATION

Next in our series of overlays are the end-times passages in the gospel of Mark. The overlay with Revelation begins with Mark 13:6 and continues uninterrupted through verse 27. Beginning in verse 28 and concluding at the end of the chapter, Jesus finishes his discussion of the signs of his coming and the end of the age with general statements of timing and an admonition to remain prepared.

Beginnings of Birth Pains

Mark 13:6

"Many will come in my name, saying, 'I am he!' and they will lead many astray."

Revelation 6:1-2

"Now I watched when the Lamb opened one of the seven seals, and I heard one of the four living creatures say with a voice like thunder, 'Come!' And I looked, and behold, a white horse! And its rider had a bow, and a crown was given to him, and he came out conquering, and to conquer."

Mark 13:7-8

"And when you hear of wars and rumors of wars, do not be alarmed. This must take place, but the end is not yet. For nation will rise against nation, and kingdom against kingdom."

Revelation 6:3-4

"When he opened the second seal, I heard the second living creature say, 'Come!' And out came another horse, bright red. Its rider was permitted to take peace from the earth."

Mark 13:8

"There will be earthquakes in various places; there will be famines. These are but the beginning of the birth pains."

Revelation 6:7-8

"When he opened the fourth seal, I heard the voice of the fourth living creature say, 'Come!' And I looked, and behold, a pale horse! And its rider's name was Death, and Hades followed him. And they were given authority over a fourth of the earth, to kill with sword and with famine and with pestilence and by wild beasts of the earth."

Great Tribulation of the Church

Mark 13:9-13

"But be on your guard. For they will deliver you over to councils, and you will be beaten in synagogues, and you will stand before governors and kings for my sake, to bear witness before them. And the gospel must first be proclaimed to all nations . . . And you will be hated by all for my name's sake. But the one who endures to the end will be saved."

Revelation 6:9-11; 7:9-17

"When he opened the fifth seal, I saw under the altar the souls of those who had been slain for the word of God and for the witness they had borne. They cried out with a loud voice, 'O Sovereign Lord, holy and true, how long before you will judge and avenge our blood on those who dwell on the earth?' Then they were each given a white robe and told to rest a little longer, until the number of their fellow servants and their brothers should be complete, who were to be killed as they themselves had been...

After this I looked, and behold, a great multitude that no one could number, from every nation, from all tribes and peoples and languages, standing before the throne and before the Lamb, clothed in white robes, with palm branches in their hands, and crying out with a loud voice, 'Salvation belongs to our God who sits on the throne, and to the Lamb!' And all the angels were standing around the throne and around the elders and the four living creatures, and they fell on their faces before the throne and worshiped God, saying, 'Amen! Blessing and glory and wisdom and thanksgiving and honor and power and might be to our God forever and ever! Amen.'

Then one of the elders addressed me, saying, 'Who are these, clothed in white robes, and from where have they come?' I said to him, 'Sir, you know.' And he said to me, 'These are the ones coming out of the great tribulation. They have washed their robes and made them white in the blood of the Lamb.

'Therefore they are before the throne of God,
     and serve him day and night in his temple; and he who
     sits on the throne will shelter them with his presence.

They shall hunger no more, neither thirst anymore;
  the sun shall not strike them, nor any scorching heat.
For the Lamb in the midst of the throne will be their shepherd,
  and he will guide them to springs of living water,
  and God will wipe away every tear from their eyes.'"

Great Tribulation of Israel

Mark 13:14-23

"But when you see the abomination of desolation standing where he ought not to be (let the reader understand), then let those who are in Judea flee to the mountains. Let the one who is on the housetop not go down, nor enter his house, to take anything out, and let the one who is in the field not turn back to take his cloak. And alas for women who are pregnant and for those who are nursing infants in those days! Pray that it may not happen in winter. For in those days there will be such tribulation as has not been from the beginning of the creation that God created until now, and never will be. And if the Lord had not cut short the days, no human being would be saved. But for the sake of the elect, whom he chose, he shortened the days." And then if anyone says to you, 'Look, here is the Christ!' or 'Look, there he is!' do not believe it. For false christs and false prophets will arise and perform signs and wonders, to lead astray, if possible, the elect. But be on guard; I have told you all things beforehand."

Revelation 12:6; 13-16

"And the woman fled into the wilderness, where she has a place prepared by God, in which she is to be nourished for 1,260 days…

And when the dragon saw that he had been thrown down to the earth, he pursued the woman who had given birth to the male child. But the woman was given the two wings of the great eagle so that she might fly from the serpent into the wilderness, to the place where she is to be nourished for a time, and times, and half a time. The serpent poured water like a river out of his mouth after the woman, to sweep her away with a flood. But the earth came to the help of the woman, and the earth opened its mouth and swallowed the river that the dragon had poured from his mouth."

Heavenly Powers Shaken, Stars / Angels Fall

Mark 13:24-25

"But in those days, after that tribulation, the sun will be darkened, and the moon will not give its light, and the stars will be falling from heaven, and the powers in the heavens will be shaken."

Revelation 12:10-11

"Now war arose in heaven, Michael and his angels fighting against the dragon. And the dragon and his angels fought back, but he was defeated, and there was no longer any place for them in heaven. And the great dragon was thrown down, that ancient serpent, who is called the devil and Satan, the deceiver of the whole world—he was thrown down to the earth, and his angels were thrown down with him. And I heard a loud voice in heaven, saying, 'Now the salvation and the power and the kingdom of our God and the authority of his Christ have come, for the accuser of our brothers has been thrown down, who accuses them day and night before our God. And they have conquered him by the blood of the Lamb and by the word of their testimony, for they loved not their lives even unto death.'"

Son of Man in the Clouds Gathering / Harvesting His Elect

Mark 13:26-27

"And then they will see the *Son of Man coming in clouds* with great power and glory. And then he will send out the angels and *gather his elect* from the four winds, from the ends of the earth to the ends of heaven." (emphasis mine)

Revelation 14:14-16

"Then I looked, and behold, a white cloud, and seated *on the cloud one like a son of man*, with a golden crown on his head, and a sharp sickle in his hand. And another angel came out of the temple, calling with a loud voice to him who sat on the cloud, 'Put in your sickle, and reap, for the hour to reap has come, for the harvest of the earth is fully ripe.' So *he who sat on the cloud swung his sickle across the earth, and the earth was reaped.*" (emphasis mine)

The Chronological Overlay of
LUKE ON REVELATION

Third in our series of overlays are the prophetic end-times passages in the gospel of Luke. The overlay with Revelation begins with Luke 21:8 and continues uninterrupted to the end of the chapter.

Beginnings of Birth Pains

Luke 21:8

"And he said, 'See that you are not led astray. For many will come in my name, saying, "I am he!" and, "The time is at hand!" Do not go after them.'"

Revelation 6:1-2

"Now I watched when the Lamb opened one of the seven seals, and I heard one of the four living creatures say with a voice like thunder, 'Come!' And I looked, and behold, a white horse! And its rider had a bow, and a crown was given to him, and he came out conquering, and to conquer."

Luke 21:9-10

"'And when you hear of wars and tumults, do not be terrified, for these things must first take place, but the end will not be at once.' Then he said to them, 'Nation will rise against nation, and kingdom against kingdom.'"

Revelation 6:3-4

"When he opened the second seal, I heard the second living creature say, 'Come!' And out came another horse, bright red. Its rider was permitted to take peace from the earth."

Luke 21:11

"There will be great earthquakes, and in various places famines and pestilences."

Revelation 6:7-8

"When he opened the fourth seal, I heard the voice of the fourth living creature say, 'Come!' And I looked, and behold, a pale horse! And its rider's name was Death, and Hades followed him. And they were given authority over a fourth of the earth, to kill with sword and with famine and with pestilence and by wild beasts of the earth."

Great Tribulation of the Church

Luke 21:12-14

"But before all this they will lay their hands on you and persecute you, delivering you up to the synagogues and prisons, and you will be brought before kings and governors for my name's sake. This will be your opportunity to bear witness. . . You will be delivered up even by parents and brothers and relatives and friends, and some of you they will put to death. You will be hated by all for my name's sake. But not a hair of your head will perish. By your endurance you will gain your lives. This will be your opportunity to bear witness. Settle it therefore in your minds not to meditate beforehand how to answer."

Revelation 6:9-11; 7:9-17

"When he opened the fifth seal, I saw under the altar the souls of those who had been slain for the word of God and for the witness they had borne. They cried out with a loud voice, 'O Sovereign Lord, holy and true, how long before you will judge and avenge our blood on those who dwell on the earth?' Then they were each given a white robe and told to rest a little longer, until the number of their fellow servants and their brothers should be complete, who were to be killed as they themselves had been...

After this I looked, and behold, a great multitude that no one could number, from every nation, from all tribes and peoples and languages, standing before the throne and before the Lamb, clothed in white robes, with palm branches in their hands, and crying out with a loud voice, 'Salvation belongs to our God who sits on the throne, and to the Lamb!' And all the angels were standing around the throne and around the elders and the four living creatures, and they fell on their faces before the throne and worshiped God, saying, 'Amen! Blessing and glory and wisdom and thanksgiving and honor and power and might be to our God forever and ever! Amen.'

Then one of the elders addressed me, saying, 'Who are these, clothed in white robes, and from where have they come?' I said to him, 'Sir, you know.' And he said to me, 'These are the ones coming out of the great tribulation. They have washed their robes and made them white in the blood of the Lamb.

'Therefore they are before the throne of God,
    and serve him day and night in his temple; and he who sits
    on the throne will shelter them with his presence.
They shall hunger no more, neither thirst anymore;
    the sun shall not strike them, nor any scorching heat.
For the Lamb in the midst of the throne will be their shepherd,
    and he will guide them to springs of living water,
    and God will wipe away every tear from their eyes.'"

Great Tribulation of Israel

Luke 21:20-24

"But when you see Jerusalem surrounded by armies, then know that its desolation has come near. Then let those who are in Judea flee to the mountains, and let those who are inside the city depart, and let not those who are out in the country enter it, for these are days of vengeance, to fulfill all that is written. Alas for women who are pregnant and for those who are nursing infants in those days! For there will be great distress upon the earth and wrath against this people. They will fall by the edge of the sword and be led captive among all nations, and Jerusalem will be trampled underfoot by the Gentiles, until the times of the Gentiles are fulfilled."

Revelation 12:6; 13-16

"And the woman fled into the wilderness, where she has a place prepared by God, in which she is to be nourished for 1,260 days. . . And when the dragon saw that he had been thrown down to the earth, he pursued the woman who had given birth to the male child. But the woman was given the two wings of the great eagle so that she might fly from the serpent into the wilderness, to the place where she is to be nourished for a time, and times, and half a time. The serpent poured water like a river out of his mouth after the woman, to sweep her away with a flood. But the earth came to the help of the woman, and the earth opened its mouth and swallowed the river that the dragon had poured from his mouth."

Heavenly Powers Shaken, Stars / Angels Fall

Luke 21:25-26

"And there will be signs in sun and moon and stars, and on the earth distress of nations in perplexity because of the roaring of the sea and the waves, people fainting with fear and with foreboding of what is coming on the world. For the powers of the heavens will be shaken."

Revelation 12:7-11
"Now war arose in heaven, Michael and his angels fighting against the dragon. And the dragon and his angels fought back, but he was defeated, and there was no longer any place for them in heaven. And the great dragon was thrown down, that ancient serpent, who is called the devil and Satan, the deceiver of the whole world—he was thrown down to the earth, and his angels were thrown down with him. And I heard a loud voice in heaven, saying, 'Now the salvation and the power and the kingdom of our God and the authority of his Christ have come, for the accuser of our brothers has been thrown down, who accuses them day and night before our God. And they have conquered him by the blood of the Lamb and by the word of their testimony, for they loved not their lives even unto death.'"

Son of Man in the Clouds Gathering / Harvesting His Elect

Luke 21:27-28
"And then they will see the *Son of Man coming in a cloud* with power and great glory. Now when these things begin to take place, straighten up and raise your heads, because your *redemption is drawing near.*" (emphasis mine)

Revelation 14:14-16
"Then I looked, and behold, a white cloud, and *seated on the cloud one like a son of man*, with a golden crown on his head, and a sharp sickle in his hand. And another angel came out of the temple, calling with a loud voice to him who sat on the cloud, 'Put in your sickle, and reap, for the hour to reap has come, for the harvest of the earth is fully ripe.' So *he who sat on the cloud swung his sickle across the earth, and the earth was reaped.*"

appendix E
THE CHRONOLOGICAL CONSISTENCY OF THE PROPHETS

This section illustrates the organizational structure of various prophetic passages as they are overlaid onto the events in the book of Revelation. Whether organized as a group of verses, chapters, or groups of chapters, key verses have been listed in chronological order along with their corresponding events from Revelation.

As we walk through these prophetic books, we begin to see God's intentional chronological organization of prophecy, not just in Revelation but throughout Scripture as concerns the time of the end and as revealed to God's prophets over hundreds of years. Although this pattern may not encompass entire books or chapters, or provide the complete pattern every time, when dealing with the end times this pattern is consistent whether in whole or part:

- National Israel Returns

- Beginnings of Birth Pains

- Great Tribulation and Apostasy of the Church

- God's Restrained Wrath

- Israel's Call to Repentance

- Great Tribulation of Israel – Beast Rule Begins

- Harvest of the Earth
- Yom Kippur - Israel's Repentance and Day of Atonement
- God's Unrestrained Wrath (Grape Harvest)
- Marriage Supper of the Lamb—Christ's Second Coming
- Thousand Year Reign of Christ
- Final Judgment / New Heaven-New Earth-New Jerusalem

The following scriptural selections revealing this pattern is incomplete, as I believe the depth of Scripture is limitless to the human mind and additional examples of its organization are yet to be discovered. The joy of discovering God's purpose in the Scriptures is one of the greatest one can have. I hope you will spend the time yourself to let God reveal the truth of Scripture to you.

The Chronological Overlay of
ISAIAH ON REVELATION

While there are other passages throughout Isaiah that apply to the time of the end, the chronological overlay of Isaiah's prophetic passages begins in Chapter 63. Isaiah's chronology is unique in that, from Isaiah 63 on, each chapter repeats an internal chronological pattern.

Chapter 63's order is maintained by recognizing that Israel's redemption is recounted in verses seven through fourteen, placing her redemption prior to the discussion of the treading of the winepress (the grape harvest) in verses one through six. The chronology included in these chapters, extending to the end of the book, covers the events in Revelation from Israel's redemption at Yom Kippur to the new heaven and new earth.

Grape Harvest
(Treading of the Winepress)

Isaiah 63:1-6
"Who is this who comes from Edom,
    in crimsoned garments from Bozrah,

he who is splendid in his apparel,
marching in the greatness of his strength?
'It is I, speaking in righteousness,
mighty to save.'
Why is your apparel red,
and your garments like his who treads in the winepress?
'I have trodden the winepress alone,
and from the peoples no one was with me;
I trod them in my anger
and trampled them in my wrath;
their lifeblood spattered on my garments,
and stained all my apparel.
For the day of vengeance was in my heart,
and my year of redemption had come.
I looked, but there was no one to help;
I was appalled, but there was no one to uphold;
so my own arm brought me salvation,
and my wrath upheld me.
I trampled down the peoples in my anger;
I made them drunk in my wrath,
and I poured out their lifeblood on the earth.'"

Isaiah Recounts Israel's Atonement
(prior to Grape Harvest)

Isaiah 63:7-14

"I will recount the steadfast love of the Lord,
the praises of the Lord,
according to all that the Lord has granted us,
and the great goodness to the house of Israel
that he has granted them according to his compassion,
according to the abundance of his steadfast love.
For he said, 'Surely they are my people,
children who will not deal falsely.'
And he became their Savior.

In all their affliction he was afflicted,
  and the angel of his presence saved them;
in his love and in his pity he redeemed them;
    he lifted them up and carried them all the days of old.
But they rebelled
  and grieved his Holy Spirit;
therefore he turned to be their enemy,
  and himself fought against them.
Then he remembered the days of old,
  of Moses and his people.
Where is he who brought them up out of the sea
  with the shepherds of his flock?
Where is he who put in the midst of them
  his Holy Spirit,
who caused his glorious arm
  to go at the right hand of Moses,
who divided the waters before them
  to make for himself an everlasting name,
  who led them through the depths?
Like a horse in the desert,
  they did not stumble.
Like livestock that go down into the valley,
  the Spirit of the Lord gave them rest.
So you led your people,
  to make for yourself a glorious name."

Israel Repents—Calls for God to Reveal Himself

Isaiah 64:1-7
"Oh that you would rend the heavens and come down,
    that the mountains might quake at your presence—
as when fire kindles brushwood
  and the fire causes water to boil—
to make your name known to your adversaries,
  and that the nations might tremble at your presence!

When you did awesome things that we did not look for,
    you came down, the mountains quaked at your presence.
From of old no one has heard
    or perceived by the ear,
no eye has seen a God besides you,
    who acts for those who wait for him.
You meet him who joyfully works righteousness,
    those who remember you in your ways.
Behold, you were angry, and we sinned;
    in our sins we have been a long time, and shall we be saved?
We have all become like one who is unclean,
    and all our righteous deeds are like a polluted garment.
We all fade like a leaf,
    and our iniquities, like the wind, take us away.
There is no one who calls upon your name,
    who rouses himself to take hold of you;
for you have hidden your face from us,
    and have made us melt in the hand of our iniquities."

Yom Kippur—Israel's Day of Atonement

Isaiah 64:8-12

"But now, O Lord, you are our Father;
    we are the clay, and you are our potter;
    we are all the work of your hand.
Be not so terribly angry, O Lord,
    and remember not iniquity forever.
    Behold, please look, we are all your people.
Your holy cities have become a wilderness;
    Zion has become a wilderness,
    Jerusalem a desolation.
Our holy and beautiful house,
    where our fathers praised you,
has been burned by fire,

and all our pleasant places have become ruins.
Will you restrain yourself at these things, O Lord?
Will you keep silent, and afflict us so terribly?"

Great Tribulation of Israel

Isaiah 65:1-7

"I was ready to be sought by those who did not ask for me;
I was ready to be found by those who did not seek me.
I said, 'Here I am, here I am,'
to a nation that was not called by my name.
I spread out my hands all the day
to a rebellious people,
who walk in a way that is not good,
following their own devices;
a people who provoke me
to my face continually,
sacrificing in gardens
and making offerings on bricks;
who sit in tombs,
and spend the night in secret places;
who eat pig's flesh,
and broth of tainted meat is in their vessels;
who say, 'Keep to yourself,
do not come near me, for I am too holy for you.'
These are a smoke in my nostrils,
a fire that burns all the day.
Behold, it is written before me:
'I will not keep silent, but I will repay;
I will indeed repay into their lap
both your iniquities and your fathers' iniquities together,
says the Lord;
because they made offerings on the mountains
and insulted me on the hills,

I will measure into their lap
   payment for their former deeds.'"

Yom Kippur—Israel's Day of Atonement

Isaiah 65:8-10

"Thus says the Lord:
'As the new wine is found in the cluster,
   and they say, "Do not destroy it,
   for there is a blessing in it,"
so I will do for my servants' sake,
   and not destroy them all.
I will bring forth offspring from Jacob,
   and from Judah possessors of my mountains;
my chosen shall possess it,
   and my servants shall dwell there.
Sharon shall become a pasture for flocks,
   and the Valley of Achor a place for herds to lie down,
   for my people who have sought me.'"

Grape Harvest (Treading of the Winepress)

Isaiah 65:11-16

"'But you who forsake the Lord,
   who forget my holy mountain,
who set a table for Fortune
   and fill cups of mixed wine for Destiny,
I will destine you to the sword,
   and all of you shall bow down to the slaughter,
because, when I called, you did not answer;
   when I spoke, you did not listen,
but you did what was evil in my eyes
   and chose what I did not delight in.'
Therefore thus says the Lord God;
'Behold, my servants shall eat,

but you shall be hungry;
behold, my servants shall drink,
    but you shall be thirsty;
behold, my servants shall rejoice,
    but you shall be put to shame;
behold, my servants shall sing for gladness of heart,
    but you shall cry out for pain of heart
    and shall wail for breaking of spirit.'
You shall leave your name to my chosen for a curse,
    and the Lord God will put you to death,
    but his servants he will call by another name.
So that he who blesses himself in the land
    shall bless himself by the God of truth,
and he who takes an oath in the land
    shall swear by the God of truth;
because the former troubles are forgotten
    and are hidden from my eyes."

Thousand-Year Reign of Christ

Isaiah 65:1-7

"For behold, I create new heavens
    and a new earth,
and the former things shall not be remembered
    or come into mind.
But be glad and rejoice forever
    in that which I create;
for behold, I create Jerusalem to be a joy,
    and her people to be a gladness.
I will rejoice in Jerusalem
    and be glad in my people;
no more shall be heard in it the sound of weeping
    and the cry of distress.
No more shall there be in it

an infant who lives but a few days,
    or an old man who does not fill out his days,
for the young man shall die a hundred years old,
    and the sinner a hundred years old shall be accursed.
They shall build houses and inhabit them;
    they shall plant vineyards and eat their fruit.
They shall not build and another inhabit;
    they shall not plant and another eat;
for like the days of a tree shall the days of my people be,
    and my chosen shall long enjoy the work of their hands.
They shall not labor in vain
    or bear children for calamity,
for they shall be the offspring of the blessed of the Lord,
    and their descendants with them.
Before they call I will answer;
    while they are yet speaking I will hear.
The wolf and the lamb shall graze together;
    the lion shall eat straw like the ox,
    and dust shall be the serpent's food.
They shall not hurt or destroy
    in all my holy mountain,'
says the Lord."

Prelude to Revelation: National Israel Returns

Isaiah 66:1-11

"Thus says the Lord:
'Heaven is my throne,
    and the earth is my footstool;
what is the house that you would build for me,
    and what is the place of my rest?
All these things my hand has made,
    and so all these things came to be,
declares the Lord.

But this is the one to whom I will look:
 he who is humble and contrite in spirit
 and trembles at my word.
'He who slaughters an ox is like one who kills a man;
 he who sacrifices a lamb, like one who breaks a dog's neck;
he who presents a grain offering, like one who offers pig's blood;
 he who makes a memorial offering of frankincense, like one who
blesses an idol.
These have chosen their own ways,
 and their soul delights in their abominations;
I also will choose harsh treatment for them
 and bring their fears upon them,
because when I called, no one answered,
 when I spoke, they did not listen;
but they did what was evil in my eyes
 and chose that in which I did not delight.'
Hear the word of the Lord,
 you who tremble at his word:
'Your brothers who hate you
 and cast you out for my name's sake
have said, "Let the Lord be glorified,
 that we may see your joy";
 but it is they who shall be put to shame.
'The sound of an uproar from the city!
 A sound from the temple!
The sound of the Lord,
 rendering recompense to his enemies!
'Before she was in labor
 she gave birth;
before her pain came upon her
 she delivered a son.
Who has heard such a thing?
 Who has seen such things?

Shall a land be born in one day?
    Shall a nation be brought forth in one moment?
For as soon as Zion was in labor
    she brought forth her children.
Shall I bring to the point of birth and not cause to bring forth?'
    says the Lord;
'shall I, who cause to bring forth, shut the womb?'
    says your God.
'Rejoice with Jerusalem, and be glad for her,
    all you who love her;
rejoice with her in joy,
    all you who mourn over her;
that you may nurse and be satisfied
    from her consoling breast;
that you may drink deeply with delight
    from her glorious abundance.'"

Yom Kippur—Israel's Day of Atonement

Isaiah 66:12-14

"For thus says the Lord:
'Behold, I will extend peace to her like a river,
    and the glory of the nations like an overflowing stream;
and you shall nurse, you shall be carried upon her hip,
    and bounced upon her knees.
As one whom his mother comforts,
    so I will comfort you;
    you shall be comforted in Jerusalem.
You shall see, and your heart shall rejoice;
    your bones shall flourish like the grass;
and the hand of the Lord shall be known to his servants,
    and he shall show his indignation against his enemies.'"

Grape Harvest

Isaiah 66:15-17

"For behold, the Lord will come in fire,
and his chariots like the whirlwind,
to render his anger in fury,
and his rebuke with flames of fire.
For by fire will the Lord enter into judgment,
and by his sword, with all flesh;
and those slain by the Lord shall be many.

'Those who sanctify and purify themselves to go into the gardens, following one in the midst, eating pig's flesh and the abomination and mice, shall come to an end together,' declares the Lord."

Thousand-Year Reign of Christ

Isaiah 66:18-24

"For I know their works and their thoughts, and the time is coming to gather all nations and tongues. And they shall come and shall see my glory, and I will set a sign among them. And from them I will send survivors to the nations, to Tarshish, Pul, and Lud, who draw the bow, to Tubal and Javan, to the coastlands far away, that have not heard my fame or seen my glory. And they shall declare my glory among the nations. And they shall bring all your brothers from all the nations as an offering to the Lord, on horses and in chariots and in litters and on mules and on dromedaries, to my holy mountain Jerusalem, says the Lord, just as the Israelites bring their grain offering in a clean vessel to the house of the Lord. And some of them also I will take for priests and for Levites, says the Lord.

"For as the new heavens and the new earth
that I make
shall remain before me, says the Lord,
so shall your offspring and your name remain.

From new moon to new moon, and from Sabbath to Sabbath,
all flesh shall come to worship before me,
declares the Lord.

"And they shall go out and look on the dead bodies of the men
who have rebelled against me. For their worm shall not die,
their fire shall not be quenched, and they shall be an abhorrence
to all flesh."

The Chronological Overlay of
JEREMIAH ON REVELATION

The overlay of Jeremiah's prophetic passages begins with commentary in chapters three and five describing Israel's resistance to repentance. We then see the great tribulation of Israel in chapter 30. Proceeding chronologically, chapters 31–33 all discuss Israel's repentance and atonement.

Israel's Call to Repentance

Jeremiah 3:11-13

"And the Lord said to me, 'Faithless Israel has shown herself more righteous than treacherous Judah. Go, and proclaim these words toward the north, and say,
"Return, faithless Israel,
declares the Lord.
I will not look on you in anger,
    for I am merciful,
declares the Lord;
I will not be angry forever.
Only acknowledge your guilt,
    that you rebelled against the Lord your God
and scattered your favors among foreigners under every green tree,
    and that you have not obeyed my voice,"
declares the Lord.'"

Jeremiah 5:3

"O Lord, do not your eyes look for truth?
You have struck them down,
    but they felt no anguish;
you have consumed them,
    but they refused to take correction.
They have made their faces harder than rock;
    they have refused to repent."

Great Tribulation of Israel

Jeremiah 30:7

"Alas! That day is so great
    there is none like it;
it is a time of distress for Jacob;
    yet he shall be saved out of it."

Yom Kippur—Israel's Day of Atonement

Jeremiah 31:31-37

"'Behold, the days are coming, declares the Lord, when I will make a new covenant with the house of Israel and the house of Judah, not like the covenant that I made with their fathers on the day when I took them by the hand to bring them out of the land of Egypt, my covenant that they broke, though I was their husband, declares the Lord. For this is the covenant that I will make with the house of Israel after those days, declares the Lord: I will put my law within them, and I will write it on their hearts. And I will be their God, and they shall be my people. And no longer shall each one teach his neighbor and each his brother, saying, 'Know the Lord,' for they shall all know me, from the least of them to the greatest, declares the Lord. For I will forgive their iniquity, and I will remember their sin no more.'

Thus says the Lord,

who gives the sun for light by day
    and the fixed order of the moon and the stars for light by night,
who stirs up the sea so that its waves roar—
    the Lord of hosts is his name:
"If this fixed order departs
    from before me, declares the Lord,
then shall the offspring of Israel cease
    from being a nation before me forever.'
Thus says the Lord:
'If the heavens above can be measured,
    and the foundations of the earth below can be explored,
then I will cast off all the offspring of Israel
    for all that they have done,
declares the Lord.'"

Jeremiah 32:37-38

"Behold, I will gather them from all the countries to which I drove them in my anger and my wrath and in great indignation. I will bring them back to this place, and I will make them dwell in safety. And they shall be my people, and I will be their God."

Jeremiah 33:14-16

"Behold, the days are coming, declares the Lord, when I will fulfill the promise I made to the house of Israel and the house of Judah. In those days and at that time I will cause a righteous Branch to spring up for David, and he shall execute justice and righteousness in the land. In those days Judah will be saved, and Jerusalem will dwell securely. And this is the name by which it will be called: 'The Lord is our righteousness.'"

The Chronological Overlay of
EZEKIEL ON REVELATION

In both Ezekiel 36 and 37, we see God taking action to restore Israel as a nation followed by restoring the nation spiritually. We also find in chapter 37 a reference to the millennial reign of Christ, which is the sole topic in Ezekiel 40–48. These two chapters set the stage for the chronological fulfillment of chapters 38–48 as presented below:

Prelude to Revelation: National Israel Returns

Ezekiel 36:24

"I will take you from the nations and gather you from all the countries and bring you into your own land."

Ezekiel 37:12-14

"Behold, I will open your graves and raise you from your graves, O my people. And I will bring you into the land of Israel. And you shall know that I am the Lord, when I open your graves, and raise you from your graves, O my people. And I will put my Spirit within you, and you shall live, and I will place you in your own land. Then you shall know that I am the Lord; I have spoken, and I will do it."

Yom Kippur—Israel's Day of Atonement

Ezekiel 36:25-29

"I will sprinkle clean water on you, and you shall be clean from all your uncleannesses, and from all your idols I will cleanse you. And I will give you a new heart, and a new spirit I will put within you. And I will remove the heart of stone from your flesh and give you a heart of flesh. And I will put my Spirit within you, and cause you to walk in my statutes and be careful to obey my rules. You shall dwell in the land that I gave to your fathers, and you shall be my people, and I will be your God. And I will deliver you from all your uncleannesses. And I will summon the grain and make it abundant and lay no famine upon you."

Ezekiel 37:23

"They shall not defile themselves anymore with their idols and their detestable things, or with any of their transgressions. But

I will save them from all the backslidings in which they have sinned, and will cleanse them; and they shall be my people, and I will be their God."

Armageddon—Battle on the Mountains of Israel
Ezekiel 38:16-23

"In the latter days I will bring you against my land, that the nations may know me, when through you, O Gog, I vindicate my holiness before their eyes…On that day there shall be a great earthquake in the land of Israel. The fish of the sea and the birds of the heavens and the beasts of the field and all creeping things that creep on the ground, and all the people who are on the face of the earth, shall quake at my presence. And the mountains shall be thrown down, and the cliffs shall fall, and every wall shall tumble to the ground. I will summon a sword against Gog on all my mountains, declares the Lord God. Every man's sword will be against his brother. With pestilence and bloodshed I will enter into judgment with him, and I will rain upon him and his hordes and the many peoples who are with him torrential rains and hailstones, fire and sulfur. So I will show my greatness and my holiness and make myself known in the eyes of many nations. Then they will know that I am the Lord."

Ezekiel 39:7

"And my holy name I will make known in the midst of my people Israel, and I will not let my holy name be profaned any more. And the nations shall know that I am the Lord, the Holy One in Israel."

Marriage Supper of the Lamb:
Christ's Second Coming
Ezekiel 39:17-20

"As for you, son of man, thus says the Lord God: Speak to the birds of every sort and to all beasts of the field, 'Assemble and come, gather from all around to the sacrificial feast that I am preparing for you, a great sacrificial feast on the mountains of Israel, and you shall eat flesh and drink blood. You shall eat the flesh of the mighty, and drink the blood of the princes of the earth—of rams, of lambs, and of he-goats, of bulls, all of them fat beasts of Bashan. And you shall eat fat till you are filled, and drink blood till you are drunk, at the sacrificial feast that I am preparing for you. And you shall be filled at my table with horses and charioteers, with mighty men and all kinds of warriors,' declares the Lord God."

Thousand-Year Reign of Christ

Ezekiel 37:24-28
"My servant David shall be king over them, and they shall all have one shepherd. They shall walk in my rules and be careful to obey my statutes. They shall dwell in the land that I gave to my servant Jacob, where your fathers lived. They and their children and their children's children shall dwell there forever, and David my servant shall be their prince forever. I will make a covenant of peace with them. It shall be an everlasting covenant with them. And I will set them in their land and multiply them, and will set my sanctuary in their midst forevermore. My dwelling place shall be with them, and I will be their God, and they shall be my people. Then the nations will know that I am the Lord who sanctifies Israel, when my sanctuary is in their midst forevermore."

Ezekiel 39:25-29
"Therefore thus says the Lord God: Now I will restore the fortunes of Jacob and have mercy on the whole house of Israel, and I will be jealous for my holy name. They shall forget their shame and all the treachery they have practiced against me, when they dwell securely in their land with none to make them afraid, when I have brought them back from the peoples and gathered them from their enemies' lands, and through them have vindicated my holiness in the sight of many nations. Then

they shall know that I am the Lord their God, because I sent them into exile among the nations and then assembled them into their own land. I will leave none of them remaining among the nations anymore. And I will not hide my face anymore from them, when I pour out my Spirit upon the house of Israel, declares the Lord God."

Ezekiel 40-48
(Entire chapters)

The Chronological Overlay of
DANIEL ON REVELATION

One of the books with the strongest overlap with Revelation is the book of Daniel. Many of the visions overlap one another, as well. Because of this internal overlap, the material in this section will be organized somewhat differently than the others. Rather than showing the parallels between Daniel and Revelation as a whole, it will be grouped by topic, showing multiple chronological parallels between varying sections of Daniel and their corresponding passages in Revelation. This approach results in the reuse of passages applying to multiple topics.

Beast of Revelation and the Rider on the White Horse

Daniel 2:31-33
"You saw, O king, and behold, a great image. This image, mighty and of exceeding brightness, stood before you, and its appearance was frightening. The head of this image was of fine gold, its chest and arms of silver, its middle and thighs of bronze, its legs of iron, its feet partly of iron and partly of clay.

Daniel 2:40-43
"And there shall be a fourth kingdom, strong as iron, because iron breaks to pieces and shatters all things. And like iron that

crushes, it shall break and crush all these. And as you saw the feet and toes, partly of potter's clay and partly of iron, it shall be a divided kingdom, but some of the firmness of iron shall be in it, just as you saw iron mixed with the soft clay. And as the toes of the feet were partly iron and partly clay, so the kingdom shall be partly strong and partly brittle. As you saw the iron mixed with soft clay, so they will mix with one another in marriage, but they will not hold together, just as iron does not mix with clay."

Daniel 8:21

"And the goat is the king of Greece. And the great horn between his eyes is the first king."

Global Conflict—Rider on the Red Horse

Daniel 8:3-7

"I raised my eyes and saw, and behold, a ram standing on the bank of the canal. It had two horns, and both horns were high, but one was higher than the other, and the higher one came up last. I saw the ram charging westward and northward and southward. No beast could stand before him, and there was no one who could rescue from his power. He did as he pleased and became great.

As I was considering, behold, a male goat came from the west across the face of the whole earth, without touching the ground. And the goat had a conspicuous horn between his eyes. He came to the ram with the two horns, which I had seen standing on the bank of the canal, and he ran at him in his powerful wrath. I saw him come close to the ram, and he was enraged against him and struck the ram and broke his two horns. And the ram had no power to stand before him, but he cast him down to the ground and trampled on him. And there was no one who could rescue the ram from his power."

Beast Nation Splits

Daniel 7:8

"I considered the horns, and behold, there came up among them another horn, a little one, before which three of the first horns were plucked up by the roots. And behold, in this horn were eyes like the eyes of a man, and a mouth speaking great things."

Daniel 7:24

"As for the ten horns,
out of this kingdom ten kings shall arise,
    and another shall arise after them;
he shall be different from the former ones,
    and shall put down three kings."

Daniel 8:8

"Then the goat became exceedingly great, but when he was strong, the great horn was broken, and instead of it there came up four conspicuous horns toward the four winds of heaven."

Daniel 8:22

"As for the horn that was broken, in place of which four others arose, four kingdoms shall arise from his nation, but not with his power."

Antichrist Takes Power (National)

Daniel 8:9-14

"Out of one of them came a little horn, which grew exceedingly great toward the south, toward the east, and toward the glorious land. It grew great, even to the host of heaven. And some of the host and some of the stars it threw down to the ground and trampled on them. It became great, even as great as the Prince of the host. And the regular burnt offering was taken away from him, and the place of his sanctuary was overthrown. And a host will be given over to it together with the regular burnt offering because of transgression, and it will throw truth to the ground, and it will act and prosper. Then I heard a holy one speaking, and another holy one said to the one who spoke, 'For how long is the vision concerning the regular burnt offering, the transgression that makes desolate, and the giving over of the sanctuary and host to be trampled underfoot?' And he said to me, 'For 2,300 evenings and mornings. Then the sanctuary shall be restored to its rightful state.'"

Daniel 8:23-25

"And at the latter end of their kingdom, when the transgressors have reached their limit, a king of bold face, one who understands riddles, shall arise. His power shall be great—but not by his own power; and he shall cause fearful destruction and shall succeed in what he does, and destroy mighty men and the people who are the saints. By his cunning he shall make deceit prosper under his hand, and in his own mind he shall become great. Without warning he shall destroy many. And he shall even rise up against the Prince of princes, and he shall be broken—but by no human hand."

Daniel's Seventieth Week Begins

Daniel 9:26-27

"And after the sixty-two weeks, an anointed one shall be cut off and shall have nothing. And the people of the prince who is to come shall destroy the city and the sanctuary. Its end shall come with a flood, and to the end there shall be war. Desolations are decreed. And he shall make a strong covenant with many for one week, and for half of the week he shall put an end to sacrifice and offering. And on the wing of abominations shall come one who makes desolate, until the decreed end is poured out on the desolator."

Daniel 11:31

"Forces from him shall appear and profane the temple and fortress, and shall take away the regular burnt offering. And they shall set up the abomination that makes desolate."

Great Tribulation of Israel

Daniel 7:25

"He shall speak words against the Most High,
    and shall wear out the saints of the Most High,
    and shall think to change the times and the law;
and they shall be given into his hand
    for a time, times, and half a time."

Daniel 9:27

"And he shall make a strong covenant with many for one week, and for half of the week he shall put an end to sacrifice and offering. And on the wing of abominations shall come one who makes desolate, until the decreed end is poured out on the desolator."

Daniel 9:24

"Seventy weeks are decreed about your people and your holy city, to finish the transgression, to put an end to sin, and to atone for iniquity, to bring in everlasting righteousness, to seal both vision and prophet, and to anoint a most holy place."

Daniel 11:31-35

"Forces from him shall appear and profane the temple and fortress, and shall take away the regular burnt offering. And they shall set up the abomination that makes desolate. He shall seduce with flattery those who violate the covenant, but the people who know their God shall stand firm and take action. And the wise among the people shall make many understand, though for some days they shall stumble by sword and flame, by captivity and plunder. When they stumble, they shall receive a little help. And many shall join themselves to them with flattery, and some of the wise shall stumble, so that they may be refined, purified, and made white, until the time of the end, for it still awaits the appointed time."

Daniel 12:6-7

"And someone said to the man clothed in linen, who was above the waters of the stream, "How long shall it be till the end of these wonders?" And I heard the man clothed in linen, who was above the waters of the stream; he raised his right hand and his left hand toward heaven and swore by him who lives forever that it would be for a *time, times, and half a time*, and that when the shattering of the power of the holy people comes to an end all these things would be finished." (emphasis mine)

Yom Kippur—Israel's Day of Atonement

Daniel 12:1

"At that time shall arise Michael, the great prince who has charge of your people. And there shall be a time of trouble, such as never has been since there was a nation till that time. But at that time your people shall be delivered, everyone whose name shall be found written in the book."

Antichrist Takes Power (International)

Daniel 8:25

"By his cunning he shall make deceit prosper under his hand, and in his own mind he shall become great. *Without warning he shall destroy many.* And he shall even rise up against the Prince of princes, and he shall be broken—but by no human hand." (emphasis mine)

Marriage Supper of the Lamb—
Christ's Second Coming

Daniel 2:34-35

"As you looked, a stone was cut out by no human hand, and it struck the image on its feet of iron and clay, and broke them in pieces. Then the iron, the clay, the bronze, the silver, and the gold, all together were broken in pieces, and became like the chaff of the summer threshing floors; and the wind carried them away, so that not a trace of them could be found. But the stone that struck the image became a great mountain and filled the whole earth."

Daniel 2:44-45

"And in the days of those kings the God of heaven will set up a kingdom that shall never be destroyed, nor shall the kingdom be left to another people. It shall break in pieces all these kingdoms and bring them to an end, and it shall stand forever, just as you saw that a stone was cut from a mountain by no human hand, and that it broke in pieces the iron, the bronze, the clay, the silver, and the gold. A great God has made known to the king what shall be after this. The dream is certain, and its interpretation sure."

Final Judgment

Daniel 7:9-12

"'As I looked,
thrones were placed,
     and the Ancient of Days took his seat;
his clothing was white as snow,
     and the hair of his head like pure wool;
his throne was fiery flames;
     its wheels were burning fire.

A stream of fire issued
  and came out from before him;
a thousand thousands served him,
  and ten thousand times ten thousand stood before him;
the court sat in judgment,
  and the books were opened.

'I looked then because of the sound of the great words that the horn was speaking. And as I looked, the beast was killed, and its body destroyed and given over to be burned with fire. As for the rest of the beasts, their dominion was taken away, but their lives were prolonged for a season and a time.'"

Daniel 7:26

"But the court shall sit in judgment,
  and his dominion shall be taken away,
    to be consumed and destroyed to the end."

Daniel 12:2-3

"And many of those who sleep in the dust of the earth shall awake, some to everlasting life, and some to shame and everlasting contempt. And those who are wise shall shine like the brightness of the sky above; and those who turn many to righteousness, like the stars forever and ever."

New Heaven / New Earth

Daniel 7:13-14

"I saw in the night visions,
and behold, with the clouds of heaven
  there came one like a son of man,
and he came to the Ancient of Days
  and was presented before him.
And to him was given dominion
  and glory and a kingdom,

that all peoples, nations, and languages
    should serve him;
his dominion is an everlasting dominion,
    which shall not pass away,
and his kingdom one
    that shall not be destroyed."

Daniel 7:27

"And the kingdom and the dominion
    and the greatness of the kingdoms under the whole heaven
    shall be given to the people of the saints of the Most High;
his kingdom shall be an everlasting kingdom,
    and all dominions shall serve and obey him."

The Chronological Overlay of
JOEL ON REVELATION

Beginning in the second chapter of Joel with the invasion of a great and powerful army, we can follow, without interruption, Israel's call to repentance, ultimate repentance and atonement, and protective rule of Jesus. Following the same chronology found in the book of Revelation, the book of Joel ends with the restoration of Jerusalem.

Second Woe

Joel 2:1-11

"Blow a trumpet in Zion; sound an alarm on my holy mountain! Let all the inhabitants of the land tremble, for the day of the Lord is coming; it is near, a day of darkness and gloom, a day of clouds and thick darkness! Like blackness there is spread upon the mountains a great and powerful people; their like has never been before, nor will be again after them through the years of all generations.

Fire devours before them, and behind them a flame burns. The land is like the garden of Eden before them, but behind them a desolate wilderness, and nothing escapes them.

Their appearance is like the appearance of horses, and like war horses they run. As with the rumbling of chariots, they leap on the tops of the mountains, like the crackling of a flame of fire devouring the stubble, like a powerful army drawn up for battle.

Before them peoples are in anguish; all faces grow pale. Like warriors they charge; like soldiers they scale the wall. They march each on his way; they do not swerve from their paths. They do not jostle one another; each marches in his path; they burst through the weapons and are not halted. They leap upon the city, they run upon the walls, they climb up into the houses, they enter through the windows like a thief.

The earth quakes before them; the heavens tremble. The sun and the moon are darkened, and the stars withdraw their shining. The Lord utters his voice before his army, for his camp is exceedingly great; he who executes his word is powerful. For the day of the Lord is great and very awesome; who can endure it?"

Israel's Call to Repentance

Joel 2:12-14

"'Yet even now,' declares the Lord, 'return to me with all your heart, with fasting, with weeping, and with mourning; and rend your hearts and not your garments.' Return to the Lord your God, for he is gracious and merciful, slow to anger, and abounding in steadfast love; and he relents over disaster. Who knows whether he will not turn and relent, and leave a blessing behind him, a grain offering and a drink offering for the Lord your God?"

Harvest of the Earth

Joel 2:16-17

"Gather the people. Consecrate the congregation;
  assemble the elders; gather the children,
even nursing infants. Let the bridegroom leave his room,
  and the bride her chamber.
Between the vestibule and the altar
    let the priests, the ministers of the Lord, weep
and say, 'Spare your people, O Lord,
    and make not your heritage a reproach,
    a byword among the nations.
Why should they say among the peoples,
    "Where is their God?"'"

Yom Kippur—Israel's Day of Atonement

Joel 2:18-22

"Then the Lord became jealous for his land
    and had pity on his people.
The Lord answered and said to his people,
'Behold, I am sending to you
    grain, wine, and oil,
      and you will be satisfied;
and I will no more make you
    a reproach among the nations.
'I will remove the northerner far from you,
    and drive him into a parched and desolate land,
his vanguard into the eastern sea,
    and his rear guard into the western sea;
the stench and foul smell of him will rise,
    for he has done great things.
'Fear not, O land;
    be glad and rejoice,

for the Lord has done great things!
Fear not, you beasts of the field,
for the pastures of the wilderness are green;
the tree bears its fruit;
the fig tree and vine give their full yield.'"

Grape Harvest / Marriage Supper of the Lamb— Christ's Second Coming

Joel 3:9-16
"Proclaim this among the nations:
Consecrate for war;
stir up the mighty men.
Let all the men of war draw near;
let them come up.
Beat your plowshares into swords,
and your pruning hooks into spears;
let the weak say, 'I am a warrior.'
Hasten and come,
all you surrounding nations,
and gather yourselves there.
Bring down your warriors, O Lord.
Let the nations stir themselves up
and come up to the Valley of Jehoshaphat;
for there I will sit to judge
all the surrounding nations.
Put in the sickle,
for the harvest is ripe.
Go in, tread,
for the winepress is full.
The vats overflow,
for their evil is great.
Multitudes, multitudes,
in the valley of decision!

For the day of the Lord is near
in the valley of decision.
The sun and the moon are darkened,
and the stars withdraw their shining.
The Lord roars from Zion,
and utters his voice from Jerusalem,
and the heavens and the earth quake.
But the Lord is a refuge to his people,
a stronghold to the people of Israel."

Thousand-Year Reign of Christ

Joel 3:17-21

"So you shall know that I am the Lord your God,
who dwells in Zion, my holy mountain.
And Jerusalem shall be holy,
and strangers shall never again pass through it.
'And in that day
the mountains shall drip sweet wine,
and the hills shall flow with milk,
and all the streambeds of Judah
shall flow with water;
and a fountain shall come forth from the house of the Lord
and water the Valley of Shittim.
'Egypt shall become a desolation
and Edom a desolate wilderness,
for the violence done to the people of Judah,
because they have shed innocent blood in their land.
But Judah shall be inhabited forever,
and Jerusalem to all generations.
I will avenge their blood,
blood I have not avenged,
for the Lord dwells in Zion.'"

ABOUT THE AUTHOR

David Kidd has spent a quarter of a century studying prophecy, with his prophetic understanding increasing in conjunction with his deepening theological perception of God's plan. As an architect, David has a passion to discover and share God's design for this creation from a designer's perspective. *A Chronological Revelation* is David's first book.

Printed in the United States
By Bookmasters